SCRAPS

Stylish Stash Fabric Crafts to Stitch

VERA VANDENBOSCH

Stylish Stash Fabric Crafts to Stitch

RAPS

The Taunton Press

The Taunton Press, Inc., 63 South Main Street, PO Box 5506, Newtown, CT 06470-5506
e-mail: tp@taunton.com

Executive editor: Shawna Mullen
Assistant editor: Tim Stobierski
Technical editor: Ashley Little
Production editor: Lynne Phillips
Copy editor: Betty Christiansen
Indexer: Barbara Mortenson
Art director: Rosalind Loeb Wanke
Photography editor: Erin Guinta
Cover and interior design: Stacy Wakefield Forte
Layout: Stacy Wakefield Forte
Illustrator: Andrew Logan Wanke
Photographer: Vera Vandenbosch

The following names/manufacturers appearing in *Scraps* are trademarks: Grippies®, Minwax®, Mod Podge®, OxiClean®

Library of Congress Cataloging-in-Publication Data in progress
ISBN # 978-1-62710-714-3

Printed in the United States of America
10 9 8 7 6 5 4 3 2 1

Acknowledgments

There are so many people who have helped this book come into being, and I am truly grateful to all of them.

Thank you to Jill Cohen, Marilyn Allen, the team at The Taunton Press—especially Shawna Mullen and Timothy Stobierski—Carin Scheve and Francesco Caramella at Next Door's photo studio/event space in Brooklyn, Keith Recker and James Mohn, Amy Ilias, Allison Kettlewell, Anthony Wagenseil, Edward Addeo, and the models: Louise, Cydney, Dylan, Katherine, and Billy Pilgrim (the cat).

I've had the pleasure and privilege of working with some amazing women throughout my career, and I tremendously value the time I spent with each: Lidewij Edelkoort, Dorothy Waxman, Sherri Donghia, and Suzanne Tucker.

Special thanks go to my parents, who have always supported and encouraged me, wherever life took me.

Last but not least, thank you to the loves of my life: Ozzy, Louise, and Paul.

See p. 20 to make your own Stacked Bangles!

CONTENTS

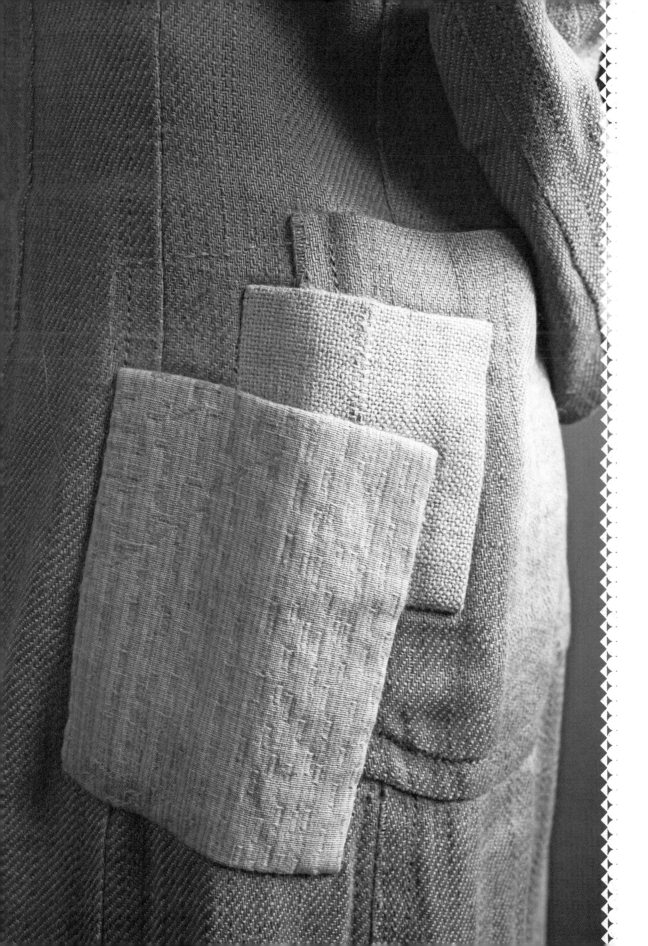

Why Scraps?

The way most people feel about throwing out perfectly good food is how I feel about throwing out textiles. *Any* textile: stained shirts, ripped jeans, stray socks, cuttings from a sewing project, or ribbons that wrapped a present. I can't tell you how many times I've picked textile items out of the trash—and thrown them straight into the washing machine.

There are so many great things you can make with all these scraps and bits that don't require stocking up on expensive craft supplies. Plus, you're reusing what you already have, rather than adding to the world's growing garbage problem. Just look around your house; you'll be amazed by what you have. Even if you're looking for specific colors or materials, a trip to the local thrift store or flea market may yield unexpected bounty.

There's no greater feeling than to tap into your own creativity and make something with your own hands. In a world that is rapidly becoming digitized and computerized, there's a unique and immeasurable value to something that's hand crafted and truly one-of-a-kind. This is why I strongly recommend *not* following the projects in this book to the exact letter, but rather taking them as a starting point for designing your very own

versions. Experimenting and adding your own personal flair is part of the process, and adults and children alike should be encouraged to follow their textile muses wherever they may take them.

Crafting in a resourceful fashion is a wonderful skill to pass on to children: It stimulates imagination, creativity, and community. The realization that creative joy and self-satisfaction are found in the process, and not solely in the finished product, is an important and encouraging lesson for young minds.

CRAFTING IN A RESOURCEFUL FASHION IS A WONDERFUL SKILL TO PASS ON TO CHILDREN.

There are no better ways to relax while spending time with friends and family than by creating something together and sharing ideas and inspiration.

Stand out from the crowd and let your personality shine by creating jewelry, accessories, and gifts that are truly yours and yours alone. Let yourself be inspired by the

latest in fashion and trends and then put your own unique spin on it. And, of course, be fashionable at your own price!

Crafting with scraps is an affordable way to update your look, your wardrobe, and your home. I've always admired the thrifty resourcefulness and sometimes sheer creative genius of Depression-era crafts. While

CRAFTING WITH SCRAPS IS AN AFFORDABLE WAY TO UPDATE YOUR LOOK, YOUR WARDROBE, AND YOUR HOME.

things have changed a lot since then, we can still learn much from the frugal approach and inventive solutions that were common in those times. With most textiles readily available at prices ranging from free to cheap, I find little reason not to gather as many as I can and just start coming up with ideas. When working with affordable materials, if something doesn't work out, that's okay!

While I never actually worked as a fashion designer (maybe one day), I did work for a long time in trend forecasting, both in Paris and New York. Then the world of home furnishings and interior design beckoned. I have always loved being part of a creative work environment, especially when textiles are involved!

Once I had children, I realized I very much wanted that creativity around them at home as well. So whenever and wherever I was able, I have always had some sort of craft project going on. I am by nature quite impatient, so not every project had a successful outcome. And that's okay: Experimenting and learning from your mistakes is very much a part of the process.

That would be my biggest tip: Enjoy the process, discover your own creativity, don't follow the rules, and, most of all, have fun!

About Me

I was born and raised just outside of Antwerp, Belgium. The nuns at the Catholic school I attended until I was 18 still believed that in addition to Latin, Greek, and science, sewing and needlework were good skills for a girl to learn, and I agree. This great academic education was followed by four years of pure creative madness at the fashion department of Royal Academy of Fine Arts.

1

MATERIALS, TOOLS, AND BASICS

A FEW SIMPLE TOOLS and whatever scraps of fabric that you can find are all you need to complete any of the projects in this book. In this chapter, I'll walk you through the best materials to use for these projects and where you can find them. You'll also learn the basic techniques that you will need to get started. It's so easy, you'll wonder why you didn't start whittling away at your scrap pile years ago!

Materials

Just look around, and you'll see you already have a treasure trove of materials in your house just waiting to be turned into amazing projects. Follow this simple rule of thumb: Never throw out anything textile-related (and I mean *anything!*) before taking a good look at it and letting your imagination run wild. This includes stained and worn-out clothing, bedding, towels, and even curtains (remember *The Sound of Music?*). Even if the color is not great, you can always dye natural materials. That brings me to my own personal exception: I do prefer to stick with natural materials such as cotton, linen, wool, and silk. They are easier to dye and overall just nicer to work with.

I often hoard materials until inspiration strikes. This can get a bit out of hand, as storage space in my house is limited, but such is the life of the crafter.

Whatever you cannot find in your own home can easily be thrifted or found online. My personal favorite search is "vintage sewing notions." You'll be amazed at what you can buy these for in bulk. And then, of course, there are yard sales, swap meets, and flea markets. I can honestly say I have never spent more than $50 during a single flea market trip, and I have always come back with a trunk full of wonderful stuff—and inspiration. I hardly ever visit a flea market

YOU ALREADY HAVE A TREASURE TROVE OF MATERIALS IN YOUR HOUSE JUST WAITING TO BE TURNED INTO AMAZING PROJECTS

with a specific shopping goal in mind, as I know I am not likely to find it. In fact, I often buy things at these markets without a very clear idea of how I will use them. The rolls of

striped grosgrain ribbon on p. 8 are a good example. They are marked "US Hat Band Mills," and, at $2 a roll, they were a steal. I know at some point inspiration will strike me.

In addition to actual fabric scraps and yardage, I am also always on the lookout for vintage lace and doilies; evening dresses that are falling apart, so that I can recycle the sequins and beads; ribbons and trim; shoelaces; buttons; zippers; broken costume jewelry—you name it. Train yourself to think outside of the box: I once found an amazing curtain tieback that I ended up wearing as a necklace. Think also in multiples: One lousy zipper is nothing special, but 300 zippers in a rainbow of colors? Now, they are just begging to be repurposed into something cool! On p. 133, I have listed some of my favorite places for thrifting and antiquing, as well as some additional stores, websites, and resources for materials and inspiration.

I also strongly suggest using social media and craft-oriented mailing lists to share your projects and ideas with friends and family, and to let your audience know you may be looking for specific materials. One man's trash is another man's treasure!

ONE LOUSY ZIPPER IS NOTHING SPECIAL, BUT 300 ZIPPERS IN A RAINBOW OF COLORS? NOW, THEY ARE JUST BEGGING TO BE REPURPOSED INTO SOMETHING COOL!

Here's a final recommendation for items that retain that stuffy thrift store smell, even after cleaning: Hang them outside during a dry, windy, and very cold day. I know, the weather needs to cooperate, but trust me, the above meteorological combination usually does the trick.

TIP Whatever material I buy that is not brand new goes straight into the washer and dryer. I am a big animal lover, but moths, fleas, and bedbugs are not welcome in my home. When cleaning delicate items such as vintage lace, I swear by the soaking method: Simply soak your items for days at a time in lukewarm water with a small scoop of OxiClean®. Stir gently and swap out the water every few hours, until it stays clean. Do not wring out the pieces; just rinse in clean water and let them dry flat on a clean towel. Refrain from using bleach: It can break down and damage fibers.

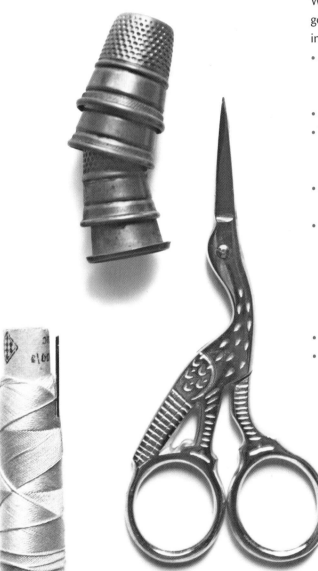

Tools

When it comes to tools, all you need is a good set of basics to get the job done. These include:

- **A good pair of fabric scissors:** Do not use these for anything other than cutting fabric.
- **A small glue gun and glue sticks**
- **Your basic sewing supplies:** A needle, thread, pins, ruler, tape measure, and thimble will come in handy.
- **A seam ripper:** You will wonder how you ever lived without one.
- **A sewing machine:** Not all projects in this book require a machine. Still, I highly recommend investing in one. Don't go for the computerized bells-and-whistles version, but rather buy a basic model in the best quality you can afford.
- **Crochet hooks**
- **Pencils and/or tailor's chalk**

Basic Techniques

HAND-STITCHED HEMS

This technique, called hemstitching, will not only come in handy for stitching a hem, but also for sewing on bias tape, patches, or appliqués, as well as any other kind of sewing that requires small, barely visible stitches.

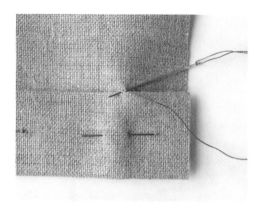

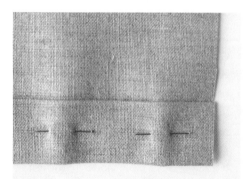

1. Prepare your work by pressing your materials and pinning your fabric—in this case, a folded hem—into place.

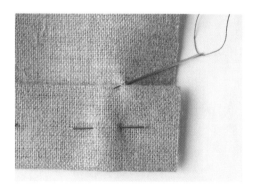

2. Thread your needle and make a double knot at the end. With your needle, pick up only one thread of your base cloth and one thread of your hem.

3. Move ¼ in. to the left and repeat. Make sure these two stitches are really close to each other and right next to the hem's edge.

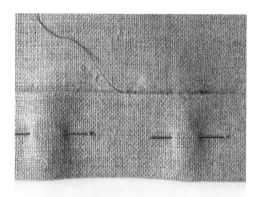

4. Repeat this process for the length of your hem. When finished, knot your thread at the end of the stitching and cut away any remaining thread.

Because you're only picking up one thread of your base cloth, the stitching will not be visible on the other side of the fabric, and because you're make tiny stitches that are very close to the hem's edge, the stitches are barely visible on that side, too, and will not come apart easily.

SQUARE CORNERS

Here are some simple tricks for sewing two pieces of fabric together to make a square corner.

2. Cut away the seam allowance in the corner diagonally, making sure you do not cut through the stitching.

1. Prepare your work by pressing both pieces of fabric and pinning them together on the marked pattern line. Machine-stitch on the pattern line and remove the pins.

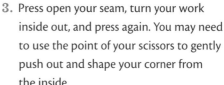

TIP **I usually machine-stitch right over my pins. If you prefer not to do that, you can temporarily baste the fabric pieces together.** *Basting* **means sewing with long, easily removable stitches by hand. If you baste, just remove the basting thread after you have machine-stitched your fabric.**

3. Press open your seam, turn your work inside out, and press again. You may need to use the point of your scissors to gently push out and shape your corner from the inside.

CONVEX CURVES

Here are some simple tricks for sewing two pieces of fabric together to make a convex curve.

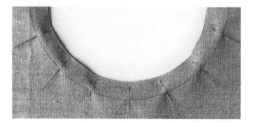

1. Prepare your work by pressing both pieces of fabric and pinning them together on the marked pattern line. Machine-stitch on the pattern line and remove the pins.

2. Make several cuts about 1 in. apart perpendicular to your stitching.

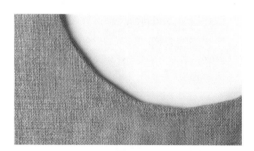

3. Press open your seam, turn work inside out, and press again. You may need to use the point of your scissors to gently push out and shape your curve from the inside.

CONCAVE CURVES

Here are some simple tricks for sewing two pieces of fabric together to make a concave curve.

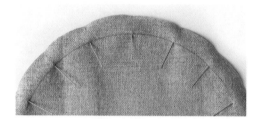

1. Prepare your work by pressing both pieces of fabric and pinning them together on the marked pattern line. Machine-stitch on the pattern line and remove the pins.

2. Make several V-shaped cuts about 1 in. apart perpendicular to your stitching.

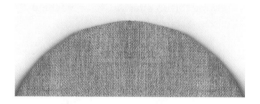

3. Press open your seam, turn work inside out, and press again. You may need to use the point of your scissors to gently push out and shape your curve from the inside.

SEWING ON BIAS TAPE

Bias tape—or bias binding—is cut on the bias, meaning its fibers are at 45 degrees to the length of the strip. This makes the tape stretchier and more malleable—and thus, the perfect tool for making a neat and beautifully finished edge, especially if your edge is curved. It's available in varying widths and a rainbow of colors. Bias tape exists in single fold and double fold. Here I have used the latter, as I wanted the color of the tape to be part of the finished edge (as seen in the Cup Holders project on p. 94).

2. Machine-stitch right where the fold is. Cut away any remaining fabric that sticks out above the tape, and fold the tape over to the other side of the piece.

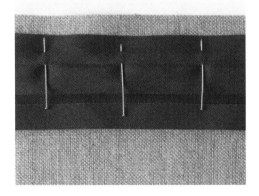

1. Fold open your bias tape and pin the crease to the outside—meaning the good side—of your item.

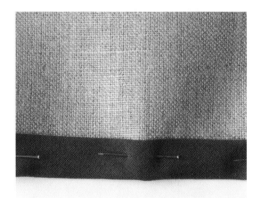

3. Pin the tape neatly in place and sew it down on the other side, using tiny hemstitches (as described on p. 12).

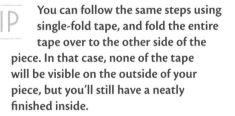

TIP You can follow the same steps using single-fold tape, and fold the entire tape over to the other side of the piece. In that case, none of the tape will be visible on the outside of your piece, but you'll still have a neatly finished inside.

CROCHET A CHAIN

The crochet chain is the foundation of any crochet work, and it's very easy to do.

1. Start by making a slipknot in the yarn.

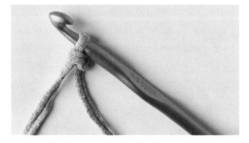

2. Stick the crochet hook through the loop of the knot and pull it tight—but not too tight.

3. Wrap the long end of the yarn over the hook from back to front.

4. Grab the yarn by turning the hook toward you and then use it to pull the yarn through the loop. You've just made your first chain stitch.

5. Keep repeating this process; practice makes perfect. To cast off your chain, simply cut off the yarn, pull the last strand all the way through the loop, and tighten.

HOW TO CROCHET

Once you've mastered the chain stitch, it's time to move on to a simple crochet stitch.

1. Crochet a chain of the desired length; this will be the width of your piece. Insert the hook through the next-to-last chain stitch.

2. Wrap the yarn back to front over the hook.

3. Grab the yarn by turning the hook toward you, and pull it through the chain stitch. Now you have two loops on your hook.

4. Wrap the yarn again over your hook, back to front.

5. Grab the yarn by turning the hook toward you, and pull it through both loops. This completes one single crochet stitch. Keep repeating this process.

6. When you get to the end of your row, make one simple chain stitch before turning your work around and starting on a new row of single stitches. To cast off your work, simply cut off the yarn, pull the last strand all the way through the last stitch, and tighten.

2 JEWELRY

I HAVE NEVER BEEN A precious-jewelry kind of girl. Not only does it scare me to own small yet pricey items that can easily disappear in the black hole that is my house, but I've always suspected that precious metals and rare gemstones may actually hinder the design process of truly creative and inspiring accessories. Take away the burden of expense, and creativity soars! This chapter will explore ideas for necklaces, bracelets, earrings, rings, corsages—all requiring a minimum of materials for a maximum of effect.

Stacked Bangles

LEVEL
Beginner—no sewing
machine required

MATERIALS
Leather or fabric
scraps
Waxed jute twine or
nylon mason line
Diamond braided
nylon cord, ⅜ in.
in diameter

**TOOLS AND
NOTIONS**
Tape measure
Scissors
Ruler
Glue gun and
glue sticks
Electrical or duct tape

The inspiration for this craft came from a famous Man Ray photo of Nancy Cunard—early 20th-century heiress, activist, and provocateur—who, it seems, never wore less than a dozen bracelets per arm, stacked all the way up to her elbows. Always make these bangles in multiples for maximum effect, and don't ask me why, but odd numbers look better than even numbers. I used a set of leather samples that were being discarded at a furniture store. Thin, supple leather works best, but experiment with color, texture, and grain to find something that fits your style.

STEPS FOR LEATHER BANGLES

1. Measure the circumference of the widest part of your fist. Add ½ in. to it, and that will be the length of your bangle.

2. Cut several pieces of diamond braided nylon cord (home improvement centers are a great source for this) in that length.

3. Cut a strip of leather ½ in. longer then the nylon cord and 1¾ in. wide. Wrap the

leather around the cord lengthwise—it will stick out a bit on one end—and secure with a glue gun. The thinner your leather is, the easier this will be.

4. When the glue has fully dried, bend the bracelet and hot-glue both ends together with the leather overlapping slightly. This is the trickiest part; depending on how pliable your leather is, you really need to hold the ends in place until the glue has fully dried. An extra pair of hands can come in handy here.

5. Secure the joint with a small piece of electrical or duct tape. Tie and wrap the waxed twine tightly around the joint so that the tape is no longer visible.

6. Keep wrapping the twine in a spiraling fashion tightly around the rest of the bracelet and secure with a double knot.

NOTE I made one bangle with fluorescent nylon mason line instead of jute. This is a little trickier, as the nylon is slippery and harder to keep in place, but I love the contrast between the organic texture of the leather and the high-tech color.

VARIATION

THE FABRIC bracelets shown here are made by wrapping a ½-in.-wide strip of cotton around the nylon rope base and hot-gluing it in place as you wrap. I used only the selvage for the blue/white bracelets, as I really liked the pattern formed by the contrast stitching on the edge. Fabric mills are a good source for selvage clippings, though store-bought printed cottons are great, too, as the selvages are often kept white and are sometimes printed with copy and color samples, which are great to incorporate into your bangles.

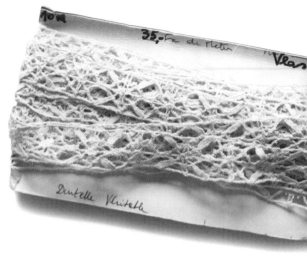

Lace Cuffs

LEVEL
Intermediate—sewing machine required

MATERIALS
Linen fabric scraps
Vintage ribbons, lace, and doilies

TOOLS AND NOTIONS
Ruler
Tape measure
Scissors
Sewing machine and thread
Pins
Needle and thread
Glue gun and glue sticks
Buttons or snaps

When I inherited my grandmother's sewing kit—she was a truly talented seamstress—I was struck by her gorgeous collection of lace and embroidery. In her time, clothing wasn't as disposable as it is today: When things finally wore out, people took great care to salvage the good bits, such as buttons, closures, lace, and embroidery, in order to reuse them in new projects. These lace cuffs are a great way to incorporate these little pieces of history into a meaningful new heirloom.

STEPS FOR CUFFS

1. Use two rectangles of fabric of the same size, preferably something heavy like a denim or sturdy linen. Mine range from 1½ in. to 2¾ in. in width. Make sure the length of the rectangle is about ½ in. more than the circumference of your wrist.

2. Machine-stitch both pieces together with a zigzag all around the edges; this will also prevent fraying.

3. Now for the fun part: Figure out how you will lay out your bits of lace and pin them down when you've found a good arrangement.

4. Attach it all to the base fabric with tiny, invisible hand stitches. If you're attaching sequins or buttons, you can also use a small dollop of hot glue.

5. For the closure, either sew one or two buttons on one side and matching thin ribbon loops on the other, or sew on snaps.

NOTE You can dye your linens and lace in strong black tea to give them even more of an antiqued look. This works best with natural materials such as silk, cotton, and linen.

VARIATION

DON'T FORGET THAT you can salvage bits and pieces from worn-out tablecloths and napkins for this project; even vintage lingerie can yield some interesting results. If you don't want to use vintage items, your local craft or fabric store will offer plenty of alternatives in terms of lace edgings, ribbons, and lace by the yard. Look for lace fabrics that contain interesting pattern elements you can cut out and appliqué.

I've made a black and gold set of cuffs as well, using a variety of sewing notions such as frog closures, gimp, and cording, as well as hex nuts and an assortment of charm hearts. For one bracelet, I simply pinned on two parallel rows of small gold safety pins.

Twisted Bracelets

LEVEL
Beginner—sewing
machine required

MATERIALS
Silk scraps
Glass bead
Ball chain
Waxed jute twine

**TOOLS AND
NOTIONS**
Tape measure
Ruler
Scissors
Sewing machine
and thread
Hand-sewing needle
(large enough
for twine)

Here's another bracelet that looks best when worn in multiples. Trust me, once you get started making these bracelets, you won't want to stop at just one! Simple materials come together for a surprising elegance that can really jazz up any outfit. They are so easy, you can make a set for every outfit in your wardrobe.

STEPS FOR TWISTED BRACELETS

1. Measure the circumference of your wrist.

2. Cut a 1-in.-wide scrap strip of textile that is about 2 in. longer than your wrist measurement. A thin silk or cotton works best. Twist the fabric strip onto itself and run a zigzag stitch over it with the sewing machine, using a matching thread color.

3. Fold over one end of your strip into a loop—large enough for your bead to pass through—and secure by wrapping waxed jute twine around it multiple times.

26

4. Position a short length of ball chain on the strip, and keep wrapping that same twine in a spiraling fashion over the strip and ball chain—placing the twine between each ball of the chain. When you get to the other end of the strip, cut off the ball chain, string a glass bead on the twine, string the twine on a needle, and secure the bead tightly by stitching it onto the end of the strip.

NOTE As a variation, you can wrap the twine around every two balls of the chain, instead of just one. For even more sparkle, try replacing the ball chain with rhinestone chain: major bling guaranteed!

Scrap Necklaces

LEVEL
Beginner—no
sewing machine
required

This is one of the easiest and quickest ways to whip up a stylish new necklace or two with a few color-coordinated fabric scraps. Contrasting textures such as linen and velvet will add even more visual interest. I love the idea of creating cool costume jewelry that is perfect for layering and almost literally an extension of the outfit you're wearing.

MATERIALS
Textile scraps
Beads
Waxed jute twine

TOOLS AND NOTIONS
Scissors
Hand-sewing needle (large enough for twine)

STEPS FOR THE LINEN/ VELVET NECKLACE

1. Cut the velvet and linen pieces into round shapes that are about twice the size of the bead diameter. There is no need to be super-precise here; in fact, the randomly shaped pieces will contribute to the overall texture of the necklace.

2. Thread your needle with the jute twine, and make a triple knot at the end. If you fear your beads will come straight off at the end, you can also tie a bead at the end of your necklace. Always leave about a 5-in. length hanging, so you have enough to tie the necklace together.

3. Wrap the linen bits around each bead and stick the needle and thread through fabric-bead-fabric, then alternate with bits of velvet that have been folded over twice. Make sure you push fabrics and beads tightly together.

4. When your necklace is the desired length—I made mine very long, as I wanted to wrap it multiple times around my neck—tie both ends together with a double knot.

VARIATION

THE RED NECKLACE—my version of a fabric lei—just alternates vintage wooden beads with knotted strips of printed quilting cotton, which are cut into ¾-in. by 4-in. pieces. I incorporated the white selvage in the fabric strips, which gives this necklace an extra graphic "pop." I have these necklaces hanging from a row of hooks over my bed, and I enjoy them just as much as room décor as jewelry. In fact, I have considered using them on my Christmas tree instead of tinsel.

Peter Pan Collar

LEVEL
Intermediate—
sewing machine
required

MATERIALS
Remnant of
embroidered fabric
1½ yd. black satin
ribbon, 1½ in. wide

**TOOLS AND
NOTIONS**
Pencil or tailor's chalk
Scissors
Pins
Paper clips
Sewing machine
and thread
Iron

Innocent and demure, the Peter Pan collar evokes feelings of childhood and nostalgia, and quite rightly so: The trend goes back as far as the early 20th century, when it was part of the Peter Pan costume in the first American production of the eponymous play. Executed in brightly colored embroidery and finished with black satin ribbons, the Peter Pan collar sheds its schoolgirl image to become quite the conversation starter.

STEPS FOR PETER PAN COLLAR

1. Using the template on p. 127, cut two collar pieces on the fold with a ½-in. seam allowance all around.

2. Pin both pieces to each other, good side to good side.

3. Cut the ribbon in two pieces, roll them both up, and insert each piece between the two pattern pieces at the front curve of the collar ends, with the length of the ribbon on the inside. A good trick is to roll up most of the ribbon length and clip it temporarily together with a paper clip, so it does not get in the way when sewing the collar. Pin the ribbon in place as well, to make sure it gets included in the seam when sewing.

4. Stitch all around the collar on the pattern line, except for a 5-in. space on the inside neck.

5. Cut off the collar's corners—making sure not to cut too close to the stitching—and make V-shaped cuts along the curved seams, as explained on p. 14.

6. Press open the seams, turn the collar inside out, and remove the paper clips from the ribbons. You can use the point of a pair of scissors to gently shape the corners from the inside.

7. Press the collar flat and hand-sew the neck opening shut with tiny stitches.

NOTE For years, I have collected any gift-wrapping ribbons discarded after the Christmas and birthday present-opening frenzy. I collect them all rolled up in a box, and this is just one of many projects where they can be put to good use. When it comes to the fabric for this project, choose one that is medium weight: Too light and the collar will not have any structure, too heavy and the corners and curves of the collar will be tricky to realize.

Bib Necklace

LEVEL
Beginner—sewing machine required

MATERIALS
Broken costume jewelry, sequins, rhinestones, brass buttons, etc.
Remnant of heavy linen canvas
Remnant of gold sequined fabric
Ribbon

TOOLS AND NOTIONS
Pencil or tailor's chalk
Scissors
Pins
Sewing machine and thread
Glue gun and glue sticks

I've always preferred larger statement necklaces over dainty little pendants. A bib necklace like this is halfway between jewelry and an item of clothing. The shape is flattering for anyone, and it will dress up the simplest of outfits. In fact, it's so much of a statement that you will want to refrain from wearing any other jewelry with it, such as earrings, bracelets, and brooches. The bib will provide all the bling you need. This project is a great way to recycle broken remains of favorite jewelry.

STEPS FOR BIB NECKLACE

1. Gather a bunch of decorative stuff that is more or less in the same color family: chains, buttons, pendants, earrings that have lost their mate, sequins, rhinestones, etc.

2. Using the template on p. 128, mark up two bib pieces with pencil or tailor's chalk, and cut out on the pattern line (no seam

allowance necessary). I prefer to match the top fabric layer with the color palette of the bib: For this gold bib, I used pieces of gold sequined fabric cut from a vintage evening dress, layered on top of a heavy linen canvas.

3. Pin the two pieces together with the good sides facing out and stitch all around, about ¼ in. from the edge, leaving the edges to fray naturally.

4. When you get to stitching the shoulder seams, first thread a piece of ribbon (20 in. to 25 in. long) between the top and bottom fabric layers, leaving one end extending out from each shoulder seam. Now, sew the shoulder seams closed, sewing through the ribbon ends. These ribbon ends will be used to tie the necklace closed.

5. Finally, here comes the fun part: Attach all your stray bits and pieces with hot glue, leaving no area uncovered. More is more!

NOTE I have found this technique really works best when you limit yourself to a color or theme. I have made versions that are entirely black mixed media or all mother-of-pearl buttons. I even made a stone version with tiny beach pebbles. Do make sure to select a heavy fabric such as canvas, corduroy, or denim as your fabric layer. Anything lighter, and your necklace will sag. You can also play with the width and shape of the bib, or make it pointy in front. Experiment!

TIP Whenever you're working with a glue gun, you'll find that your craft piece may get covered with little "threads" of glue. Ignore those while you're working. When your project has dried, they can easily be pulled off and will not affect your work.

Beads 3 Ways

TRIBAL BEADS

LEVEL
Beginner—no sewing machine required

MATERIALS
Lightweight woolen scraps (I used a vintage Russian scarf that had holes in it)

Nylon mason line

TOOLS AND NOTIONS
Ruler
Pencil or tailor's chalk
Scissors
Wallpaper paste
Wooden skewers
Strong glue

Beads are the most basic jewelry component, and they have quite a history. Trade beads were used as early as the 16th century as currency to exchange for goods and services. They were made across Europe, though colorful Venetian glass beads were especially renowned. Older bead examples date back as far as the Stone Age. Because they are such small and simple objects, they are among the easiest projects in this book—and require only a tiny bit of material—yet the design possibilities for these little objects of beauty are myriad.

STEPS FOR TRIBAL BEADS

1. Using your ruler and pencil, mark up and cut out forty 1-in.-wide strips of fabric. They should be about 13 in. long.

2. Cover both sides of each strip in wallpaper paste (I used the premixed kind), and wrap tightly around a wooden skewer (these will become the beads). This is a bit of a messy process, so make sure you do this on a well-protected surface.

3. Let the beads dry thoroughly; this will take at least four to five days.

4. Gently pry the bead off the skewer and string it on nylon cord. Make a knot in between each bead, and tie the ends of the nylon cord together to close the necklace. Use a drop of strong glue to keep the ends from fraying.

WRAPPED CANDY BEADS

LEVEL
Beginner—sewing machine required

MATERIALS
Printed cotton scraps
Uncooked rice
Waxed jute twine

TOOLS AND NOTIONS
Cardboard
Ruler
Pencil or tailor's chalk
Scissors
Sewing machine and thread

STEPS FOR WRAPPED CANDY BEADS

1. Make a cardboard template that is 3 in. by 4 in.

2. Using the template and a pencil, mark up 20 rectangles on the back side of the cotton and cut them out.

3. Fold over your rectangle lengthwise, good side on good side, and stitch together about ¼ in. from the edge.

4. Turn inside out and tie off your fabric tube at one end with a length of waxed twine.

5. Make a funnel with a bit of cardboard and fill the tube with a spoonful of uncooked rice, then tie off the other end as well.

6. Tie all the filled beads together by knotting together the twine that was also used to tie off the beads' ends.

SILK BEADS

LEVEL
Beginner—no sewing
machine required

MATERIALS
Silk scraps
5 large plain wooden
beads (mine were 1¾ in.
in diameter)

6 smaller glass beads
Shoelace

TOOLS AND NOTIONS
Scissors
Glue gun and
glue sticks

STEPS FOR SILK BEADS

1. Cut your silk into ¼-in.-wide strips.

2. Wrap and glue strips around your wooden
   bead, starting next to the bead hole and
   making sure you do not cover either of the
   bead holes.

3. When you start a new strip, wrap and glue
   in a different direction, in order to cover all
   of the bead's surface.

4. I strung my five finished beads on a vintage
   shoelace, alternating with Venetian glass
   beads, and simply knotted the ends of the
   shoelace together to close the necklace.

Braided Necklace

LEVEL
Beginner—no sewing machine required

MATERIALS
Silk, cotton scraps, or thin ribbons

TOOLS AND NOTIONS
Scissors

My daughter Louise currently has hair that is almost 3 ft. long, so I have had some serious braiding experience over the last few years. It's one of those things that is actually easier to do if you don't think about it all that much, though you do need a partner to help you out with this particular project.

STEPS FOR BRAIDED NECKLACE

1. Rip your fabric into three long ½-in.-wide strips. A good rule of thumb is that your final braid will be about one-third shorter than your original strip length, so if you want a 28-in. necklace, you should start with 42-in.-long strips. If you prefer a cleaner look, cut your fabric with scissors instead of ripping. Have your craft partner hold on to all three pieces and sit across from him or her.

2. Take the right-hand strip and place it in the middle, then take the left-hand strip and place it in the middle. Keep repeating this; it's that simple!

3. When your necklace has reached the desired length (do make sure it will fit over your head), simply knot the ends together.

NOTE These necklaces look best when layered in multiples. Try making some in a tonal palette, using different fabric textures. I made the darkest necklace in the picture with three lengths of a ¼-in.-wide satin ribbon. A word of warning, though: The thinner your ribbon or fabric, the longer the braiding will take.

Rings

LEVEL
Beginner—no sewing
machine required

MATERIALS
Small fabric scraps,
light to medium
weight (I used
a Chinese silk
embroidery, a linen
napkin, a printed
cotton, a lightweight
viscose velvet, a
viscose jacquard, a
felt, a silk foulard, and
a shantung)

**TOOLS AND
NOTIONS**
Scissors
Button-making kits
in various sizes (mine
were ¾ in. in diameter
for the smallest and
1½ in. in diameter
for the largest rings)
Ring blanks
Pliers
Small hammer
Strong glue

The cocktail ring—a large fashion statement of a ring—made its debut during the Prohibition years, when it was worn at illegal cocktail parties by women who flaunted the fact that they were drinking illegally, and doing so with panache. The cocktail ring continued to be associated with independent women, when it was believed that such a big and dramatic ring was clearly not a wedding band, but a ring a woman would buy for herself. Look for specific fabric design elements you can center on your ring: a printed flower, an embroidery element, a great color—you get the idea!

STEPS FOR RINGS

1. Follow the instructions of your button-making kit: Cut out a fabric circle following the kit's template, pop it in the mold good side down, put in the button top good side down, fold over the fabric edges, and clip on the button bottom.

2. Using a pair of pliers, gently and carefully remove the button's shank. The shank is the raised loop on the back that is used to sew on the button.

3. Here's the most important step: Make sure the back of your button is as flat as possible. If necessary, even out any bumps with a tap of a small hammer (or with the tips of your pliers).

4. Place your button, fabric side down, on a flat surface, put a drop of strong glue on the center of the back, and place the ring blank on top, disk side down. Let dry for at least a few hours before wearing.

Corsage

LEVEL
Beginner—no sewing machine required

MATERIALS
Silk scraps (¼ yd. is more than enough for one flower)

TOOLS AND NOTIONS
Pencil or tailor's chalk
Cardboard
Scissors
Wallpaper paste
Paintbrush
Aluminum soft drink cans
Knife
Small safety pin
Needle and thread
Glue gun and glue sticks

One of my earliest childhood memories involves a faded floral shoebox my mother kept on the top shelf of her wardrobe. It was only taken out on special occasions, and it contained a wonderful collection of silk flowers. Some came off my mother's wedding veil; others had been part of various communion headpieces for my sisters and me. I thought they were the most precious things, even if they were kind of frivolous and a tad old-fashioned. Here's how to make your own.

STEPS FOR CORSAGE

1. Using the template on p. 129, make a cardboard template for your flower petal, and cut out 16 silk petals (no need for a seam allowance).

2. Brush wallpaper paste (I use the premixed kind) onto the front and back of each petal, making sure the fabric is completely soaked through, except for the bottom "tab" of the petal, which should be kept paste-free.

3. Place your petals horizontally onto your aluminum cans to dry (don't overlap them); this will take about a day.

4. Once fully dried, pry the petals off with the tip of a knife.

5. Make a crease where the petal meets the tab.

6. Sew the safety pin to the back of your first petal's tab; this will be your bottom petal.

7. Once this is done, hot-glue your second petal's tab on top of the first tab, with the petal itself facing the other direction.

8. Keep stacking and gluing petals on top, always varying the petals' position.

NOTE For the best results, use a lightweight fabric. A silk shantung or satin will give your flowers a pretty sheen, but you can also use a lightweight cotton or linen and experiment with patterned textiles as well.

Lace Earrings

LEVEL
Beginner—no sewing machine required

MATERIALS
Small fragments of lace and/or crochet pieces

TOOLS AND NOTIONS
Scissors
Mod Podge®
Paintbrush
Plastic lid
Needle
Gold and/or silver paint (I used the kind meant for painting model cars)
Earring hooks
Jump rings
Pliers

The inspiration for this project came from antique filigree metalwork. It occurred to me that the delicate detailing of heavy guipure lace and crochet is very reminiscent of this technique. Thus, these dramatic chandelier earrings were born, and the beauty is that they're quite lightweight, so easy to wear, and a cinch to make.

STEPS FOR EARRINGS

1. Cut out the fragment of lace or crochet that will make up your earring; don't worry about fraying ends—the Mod Podge will prevent any unraveling.

2. Brush a thick layer of Mod Podge on both front and back, and lay the lace on a flat plastic lid to dry. Dab the tip of your brush onto the lace to make the details in the lace pop.

3. Once the Mod Podge has fully dried (this can take up to 24 hours), gently pry the lace fragment from the plastic lid by bending it.

4. Use a needle to punch through any lace bits that may have accidentally been painted "shut" by the Mod Podge, and to poke a hole near the top of the earring.

5. Paint the front and back of the lace fragment gold (or silver) and let dry.

6. Attach the fragment to an earring hook with a jump ring, using a pair of pliers.

NOTE You can also layer different lace fragments together in one earring, which is what I did for the smallest one in the picture: I cut out three different fragments from the same lace ribbon, and they are all attached to the earring hook with one single jump ring.

T-Jewelry

LEVEL
Beginner—no sewing machine required

MATERIALS
T-shirts

TOOLS AND NOTIONS
Tape measure
Ruler
Scissors
Crochet hook size M/13 (9 mm)
24 key chain clips, 1½ in. long
24 hex nuts, ½ in. in diameter
Brass compression sleeves, ½ in. in diameter
Clear tape
Needle and thread
Diamond braided nylon rope, ⅜ in. in diameter

To make your own T-shirt yarn, lay your T-shirt flat and cut off the bottom hem. Cut in a straight line from armpit to armpit. Place the tube of fabric flat on a table and cut ¾-in.-wide strips horizontally from left to right, stopping 1 in. from the right edge (see diagram 1 on p. 129). Once all your cuts have been made, pick up your fabric tube, stick your arm through it and under the part that has not been cut through. Now, instead of continuing your cuts straight across, connect your cuts diagonally to the left side (see diagram 2 on p. 129). You will end up with one long piece of T-shirt yarn, which you can roll up like a ball and use to make this fun jewelry!

STEPS FOR THE BLACK NECKLACE

1. Using your T-shirt yarn, start a simple crochet chain of 8 stitches, making sure there is a length of at least 10 in. at the end of the chain. See p. 16 for instructions on how to crochet a chain.

2. Now, keep making the crochet chain, but include the loop of a keychain clip in each stitch. Do this for the next 24 stitches. Finally, crochet 8 more chain stitches and cast off by pulling the end of your yarn through your loop, leaving another end that is at least 10 in.

3. For each tassel, cut five 6-in. pieces, thread them all together through the clip of each keychain, fold over, and tie off underneath the keychain with another short piece of yarn. To close the necklace, just tie the ends together into a little bow.

STEPS FOR THE
RED NECKLACE

1. For the red necklace, make a simple crochet chain of 40 stitches and cast off by pulling the end of the yarn through the loop. Make sure there is at least 10 in. of yarn at the beginning and end of the chain.

2. Now, crochet 24 more chains that are each 13 stitches in length. Each piece should have about 7 in. of yarn at the beginning and end of the chain.

3. Take your large chain and fold it over to find the center; starting in that spot,

loop the end of one of the shorter chains through the crochet stitch and secure with a knot. Do the same thing on the left and right sides, evenly working your way out from the center to the sides, until you run out of short chains.

4. Finally, thread a hex nut onto each of the shorter chains and make a knot underneath so the hex nut is firmly secured in place. The hex nuts will give sparkle and weight to the piece.

5. To close the necklace, just tie the ends together into a little bow.

STEPS FOR THE GRAY NECKLACE

1. The gray necklace is the simplest one to make. First, use a length of yarn to decide how long you want the necklace to be—it can be any length; just make sure it will fit over your head. Mine is 28 in. long.

2. Cut 13 pieces of yarn of that same length.

3. Hold the lengths together and thread ten (more if your necklace is longer) brass compression sleeves on them. Space the rings out evenly.

4. Wrap a small piece of clear tape connecting both ends, as tightly as you can, and secure both ends together with a few stitches. Slip one of the compression sleeves over the seam to hide it from view.

NOTE You can also skip the step of cutting up T-shirts altogether and purchase ready-made T-shirt yarn from a craft store. It is available in a wide range of colors and patterns, ready for use.

3 HOME

WHEN MY HUSBAND and I purchased our Brooklyn home—more than 14 years of thrifting ago!—I had so many ideas and thoughts for how I wanted to decorate it that I started a collection of scrapbooks to keep track of them all. Even though we moved in a long time ago, I still contribute to my old scrapbooks and often look through them for inspiration. Many of the projects in this chapter were born on those pages.

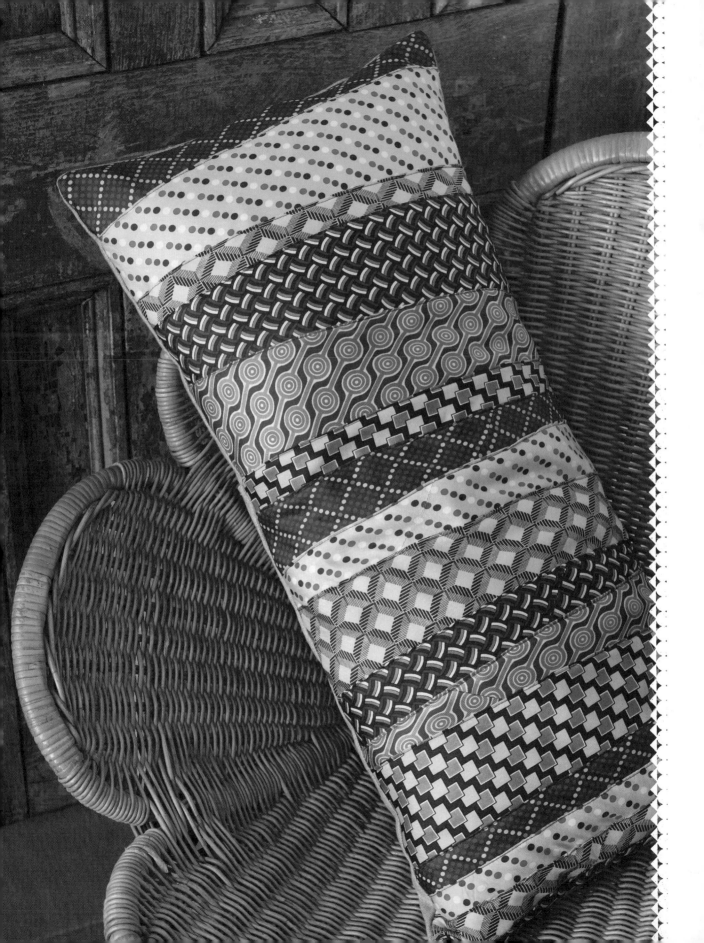

Necktie Pillow

LEVEL
Intermediate—sewing machine required

MATERIALS
6 silk men's ties
¾ yd. of medium-weight linen
Rectangular pillow insert, 12 in. by 24 in.

TOOLS AND NOTIONS
Pencil or tailor's chalk
Ruler
Scissors
Pins
Sewing machine and thread
Iron

Vintage silk ties have such wonderfully graphic patterns; they are great for mixing and matching together on a decorative bolster pillow, perfect for a midcentury modern décor. Look for the perfect combination of patterns and color at tag sales and thrift stores and let them inspire you. Because tie silk is relatively thin and fragile, I appliquéd the ties to a linen background before incorporating them into my pillow. Groovy, baby!

STEPS FOR NECKTIE PILLOW

1. Using pencil and ruler, mark an 11-in. by 23-in. rectangle on the linen, and cut out with a ½-in. seam allowance all around.

2. Cut the ties into 12-in.-long pieces. There is no need to undo the stitching of the ties or to remove any lining.

3. Pin the first piece on the good side—meaning the unmarked side—of the linen rectangle, starting on the left side. Make sure the tie piece overlaps with the seam allowance.

4. Now pin the second piece on, making sure it overlaps slightly with the first tie. Since the ties are decreasing in width, you will

need to alternate directions: wide to narrow, narrow to wide, wide to narrow, and so on.

5. Keep pinning until the entire surface is covered with ties.

6. Machine-stitch a straight line in every spot where two ties overlap, making sure that the stitching is as close as possible to the edge of the tie. This is somewhat tricky, as the tie silk is slippery, so do this slowly and carefully. Once all ties are stitched down, the pillow front is done.

7. Using pencil and ruler, mark two 11-in. by 26-in. rectangles on the linen, and cut out with a ½-in. seam allowance all around.

8. On one of the 11-in. sides, make a hem by folding over the linen twice, first by ½ in., then by 1 in. Press down this hem and secure with two rows of machine stitching: one right at the edge of your piece and one right at the edge of the hem. Make sure to use a thread that is the same color as your linen fabric. Repeat this process for the other 11-in. by 26-in. piece.

9. Place your pillow front on your work surface, good side up. Place both pillow backs on top, good side down, aligning the edges. They will overlap in the middle.

10. Pin all pieces together, and machine-stitch all around. Remove the pins.

11. Carefully cut off the seam corners diagonally (as shown on p. 13), making sure not to cut into the stitching.

12. Press open the seams and turn the pillow cover inside out. Gently push out and shape each corner with the point of your scissors from the inside. Press flat with an iron and stuff with the pillow insert.

NOTE Once you've mastered this project, think of all the other things you could appliqué on a fabric surface and turn into a unique pillow: vintage handkerchiefs, pocket squares, doilies . . .

Egg Hats

LEVEL
Beginner—no
sewing machine
required

MATERIALS
Stray baby socks
Yarn remnants

**TOOLS AND
NOTIONS**
Scissors
Needle and thread
Pom-pom maker
(optional)

As a kid, I loved soft-boiled eggs with "soldiers." Soldiers are little strips of toast you can dunk into the yellow, drippy egg yolk. It's not big in American to-go culture, but more appropriate for a proper sit-down breakfast. When I was young, we used egg hats to keep the eggs warm until everyone was at the table. Egg hats make me think of Easter and spring and long, drawn-out Sunday breakfasts.

STEPS FOR EGG HATS

1. Cut off the foot of your baby sock, so you are left with a piece of knit tube. Thread your needle and make a double knot at the end.

2. Make a small running stitch at the unfinished end of the sock, cinch together, turn the unfinished edge to the inside of the sock, and secure with a few more stitches. Don't cut off the thread just yet.

3. Make a small 2-in. pom-pom. You can do this by just wrapping a big clump of yarn around three fingers, tying firmly together in the middle, and cutting through the ends. You can also use my new favorite craft tool: the pom-pom maker. Clover Needlecraft makes them in all sizes. Trim your pom-pom to the desired size, and securely attach it to the top of the sock with the needle and remaining thread.

NOTE As an alternative to socks, you could also use the sleeves of long-sleeved infant T-shirts and onesies for this project. The edge of the sleeve becomes the bottom of your egg hat; cut off the sleeve at the desired length, cinch, and attach a pom-pom.

Grandpa Blanket

LEVEL
Intermediate—
sewing machine
required

MATERIALS
4 extra-large
men's flannel shirts in
a variety of patterns
2 yd. medium-
to heavyweight
cotton (for
the backing)
54 buttons

**TOOLS AND
NOTIONS**
Cardboard
Pencil or tailor's chalk
Scissors
Pins
Sewing machine
and thread
Iron
Needle and thread

During the Great Depression, quilts were made from just about any fabric that was available: worn-out blankets, feed sacks, even cigar box ribbons. I love the ingenuity of repurposing one thing to make another, and I like it even more when there is an emotional connection. Thus, I came up with the Grandpa Blanket, made from the discarded flannel shirts from a favorite grandpa, father, uncle . . . you name it.

STEPS FOR GRANDPA BLANKET

1. Make a cardboard template that is a 6-in. square. Use this template to mark up 70 pieces of flannel from 4 shirts (you should get between 17 to 18 squares per shirt), and cut them out with a ½-in. seam allowance all around.

2. Lay your pieces—good side up—in a seven-by-ten grid on the floor, and decide which

61

layout works best. I decided to lay out my colors in a diagonal pattern.

3. Once you have determined your layout, start by pinning the seven pieces in each row together—good side to good side—and stitch them together on your sewing machine.

4. Press open the seams on the back of each of the 10 strips you now have.

5. Now, pin your 10 rows together—again good side to good side—and stitch them together on your sewing machine. Press open the seams on the back. This completes the front of the blanket.

6. Mark up a 42-in. by 60-in. rectangle on the bad side of your backing fabric, and cut out with a ½-in. seam allowance all around.

7. Lay your blanket front on the floor—good side up—and place your blanket back on top of it—good side down. Pin together and machine-stitch all around, leaving a 20-in. opening in the middle of one side. Remove the pins.

8. Carefully cut off the seam corners diagonally (as shown on p. 13), making sure not to cut into the stitching.

9. Press open seams and turn the blanket inside out. Gently push out and shape each corner with the point of your scissors from the inside. Press flat with an iron, then pin and hand-stitch the opening shut. Remove the pins.

10. Once again, place the blanket flat on the floor, with the flannel side facing up. Make sure both layers are smoothed out.

11. Now pin both layers—flannel front and backing cotton—together at each point where the flannel squares meet. Sew a button on each of those spots—that's 54 buttons in total, and you are done. *Phew!*

NOTE Of course, this blanket could be made out of a variety of items that you'd like to turn into a keepsake. When shopping for a backing fabric, make sure to pick one that is either equal to or slightly heavier in weight than the front.

Lamp-shade

LEVEL
Beginner—no sewing machine required

MATERIALS
Lightweight printed cotton
Plain paper lampshade

TOOLS AND NOTIONS
Scissors
Mod Podge
Paintbrush

It is remarkable how a simple craft intervention can turn an ordinary object from "meh" to "wow!" Case in point: this plain brown paper lampshade, purchased for a song at a local Salvation Army. It was the right color, shape, and size for my lamp base; it just lacked a certain *je ne sais quoi*. Enter Mod Podge, my new favorite craft condiment, and this beauty was born.

NOTE You will want to put some thought into the pattern placement of the shade: I opted for a concentration of butterflies on the bottom of one side, and just a few flying to the top of the shade.

STEPS FOR LAMPSHADE

1. Find a printed fabric that contains a pattern element you can cut out. I cut out butterflies. Use a pair of small, sharp scissors for this, as you want to cut out as much detail as possible.

2. Brush a coat of Mod Podge onto the back of the fabric cutout, place it onto your lampshade, and then brush a coat over the entire thing, making sure you go *over* the edges so the cutout is fully adhered.

3. Once all your cutouts have been affixed, brush another coat of Mod Podge over the entire shade; this will even out the color of the shade, which will likely turn a little bit darker with the Mod Podge. Let dry overnight before using.

NOTE You will really need to look for fabric with pattern elements that make the perfect cutout, such as birds and other animals, flowers, or geometric shapes. You can also try this technique with lightweight lace for a pretty and romantic look.

Pet Bed

LEVEL

Intermediate—sewing machine required

By now it must be obvious that I have a soft spot for craft projects, mine and other people's as well. So when I come across half-finished needlepoint pieces at the flea market, I have to buy them. Rather than actually finishing them, I've decided to incorporate them into a project as is. Your furry friends will thank you for their new, cozy little sleeping spot!

MATERIALS

Assorted pieces of needlepoint, finished or half-finished

1 yd. of heavy linen canvas

Square euro pillow insert, 28 in. by 28 in.

TOOLS AND NOTIONS

Cardboard

Pencil or tailor's chalk

Scissors

Pins

Sewing machine and thread

Iron

Spray bottle with water

STEPS FOR PET BED

1. Make a cardboard template that is a 6½-in. square. Use this template to mark up 16 pieces of needlepoint, and cut them out with a ½-in. seam allowance all around.

2. Lay your pieces—good side up—in a four-by-four grid on the floor, and decide which layout works best.

3. Once you have determined your layout, start by pinning the four pieces in each row together—good side to good side—and stitch them together on your sewing machine. Remove the pins.

4. Press open the seams on the back of each of the four strips you now have. You may want to slightly dampen your work with a spray bottle, as the needlepoint canvas is quite coarse and not easy to press.

5. Now, pin your four rows together—again good side to good side—and stitch them together on your sewing machine. Remove the pins. Press open the seams on the back. This completes the front of the pillow.

6. With your pencil, mark up two pieces of canvas that are 26 in. long by 30 in. wide and cut out with a ½-in. seam allowance. These will make up the back of your pillow.

7. On one of the 26-in. sides, make a hem by folding over the canvas twice, first by ½ in., then by 1 in. Press down this hem and secure with two rows of machine stitching: one right at the edge of your piece, and one right at the edge of the hem. Make sure to use a thread that is the same color as your linen canvas. Repeat this process for the other 26-in. by 30-in. piece.

8. Place your needlepoint pillow front on your work surface, good side up. Place both pillow backs on top, good side down, aligning the edges. They will overlap in the middle.

9. Pin all pieces together, and machine-stitch all around. Remove the pins.

10. Carefully cut off the seam corners diagonally (as shown on p. 13), making sure not to cut into the stitching.

11. Press open the seams and turn the pillow cover inside out. Gently push out and

shape each corner with the point of your scissors from the inside. Press flat with an iron and stuff with the pillow insert.

NOTE When making pillow covers, always make them 1 in. to 2 in. smaller than your pillow insert. This will make for a snug fit, and your pillow will look nice and plump! I purposefully selected sturdy materials, as this pillow was going to be used on the floor as a pet bed: Both the needlepoint canvas and the heavy linen are pretty much indestructible and can withstand much abuse. Other good fabric choices would include heavyweight denims, upholstery-weight velvets, and corduroys.

Wallpaper Paste Bowls

LEVEL
Beginner—no sewing machine required

MATERIALS
Fabric scraps—light- to medium-weight linens and cottons work best

TOOLS AND NOTIONS
Scissors
Wallpaper paste
Plastic to protect work surface
Plastic bowls or exercise ball to use for shaping
Mod Podge
Paintbrush
Paper towels

I have been crafting with papier-mâché since kindergarten, and when I developed the projects for this book, I wondered if a similar technique could be applied to textiles. The answer is yes, though I did discover that your fabric needs to have a "dry" texture such as cotton or linen. This does not work so well with slippery fabrics such as silk and satin. You can buy wallpaper paste readily mixed, or you can buy the powdered kind and mix your own. This bowl is both attention-grabbing and utilitarian; place on a side table as a convenient collection plate for keys or mail or in your living room to get the conversation flowing.

STEPS FOR WALLPAPER PASTE BOWLS

1. Cut your textile material in irregular strips and pieces. I used a cotton gauze material and even included some disintegrating vintage tulle with beading details for the inside of my bowl.

71

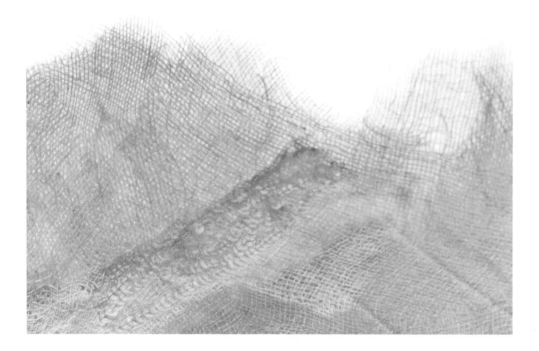

2. Coat each piece with a generous amount of paste on both sides. This is a messy process that is best done with your hands and on a well-protected work surface.

3. Place strips on a plastic bowl placed upside down, and smooth down with your hands. I used an exercise ball, as I wanted my piece to be extra-large.

4. When layering strips, make sure to crisscross and flatten them down, and squeeze out any extra paste. Your final bowl should be at least three to four layers thick. Don't worry too much about the excess glue: Wallpaper paste dries clear.

5. Now comes the hard part: Your bowl has to dry for at least three days. When you are sure it is really completely dry, it should be very easy to remove by bending your plastic shape (in my case, the exercise ball). If not, use the point of a knife to gently pry it off.

6. You can give your finished piece some extra protection by brushing on several layers of Mod Podge. If you decide to do this, do make sure to coat both inside and outside of your bowl; otherwise it might warp. Your finished pieces are meant to be decorative items, great for potpourri, dried flowers, and lightweight items, but not suitable for serving food.

TIP It is crucially important to have all your fabric pieces cut, all materials within reach, and your work surface protected with plastic. Once your hands are covered with glue, you won't be able to handle much else, and that includes phone calls. Don't panic if you have spills; wallpaper paste is water soluble and cleans off easily.

Coiled Bowls

LEVEL
Beginner—no sewing machine required

MATERIALS
Printed cotton scraps

TOOLS AND NOTIONS
Scissors
Diamond braided nylon rope, ⅜ in. in diameter
Glue gun and glue sticks
Round plastic pots/bowls/ exercise ball to use for shaping

Hardware stores have become a great and affordable craft resource for me. I often walk through the aisles looking at plumbing supplies, copper fixtures, and chains, imagining what I could make with them. I've received some weird looks from the sales associates when I explain that my hex nuts will be incorporated into a cool necklace or that my large hose clamps will be turned into stylish trivets for the dining table. When I discovered a bundle of thick nylon rope for just a few dollars, I could not resist taking it home. I made a chain bracelet (see Twisted Bracelets, p. 26) and, later, this set of bowls. Here's how.

STEPS FOR COILED BOWLS

1. Cut long ½-in.-wide strips of light- to medium-weight cotton fabric. You can also tear the strips, which will give your bowls a fuzzy, "frayed" finish.

2. Wrap the strips around your nylon rope, overlapping them slightly so no rope is visible, and secure them with little dabs of hot glue as you go. Make at least 4 yd. to 5 yd. of wrapped rope, more if you want your bowl to be extra-large.

(Continued on p. 76)

Coiled Bowls continued from p. 73

3. If you run out of a textile strip, start a new one that overlaps with the end of the previous one by about 1 in. Secure with a dab of hot glue.

4. To make the bowl, fold over the very end of your wrapped cord and secure it with glue and a few stitches. The cord is so thick that glue alone won't hold this first part together.

5. Now, keep wrapping your cord in a spiraling fashion around this first coil, securing with little dabs of hot glue between the rope as you go along. You'll want to do this part short bits at a time, holding the cords tight for a minute or so until the glue has dried—hot glue does not take very long to dry and set. It's best to do this on a clean, flat, and protected surface.

6. Once the bottom of your bowl is the desired size, you can place it on top of a plastic bowl that is placed upside down. Now, keep wrapping and gluing, following the curves of your bowl all the way down. When you've reached the desired height, cut off the rope and you're done. Don't be worried if it turns out you've glued your fabric bowl to your plastic bowl; you can easily pull it off, and once it is completely dry, you can also pull off any excess bits and threads of glue.

NOTE These fabric bowls make great gifts and are wonderful to organize jewelry and small trinkets. Of course, you can also keep the spiral flat, and you'll end up with a great-looking trivet. Or, make the spiral super-large, and you'll have a gorgeous circular rug.

VARIATION

YOU CAN USE THE SAME TECHNIQUE to create beautiful coiled pendant lampshades. Follow the steps for the coiled bowls, but before you start coiling the wrapped cord over the item you are using for shaping (I used a basketball), insert the end of a pendant lamp kit so that the socket goes through your first loop. Once your lamp is the desired shape, screw a lightbulb into the socket, and you're ready to hang the pendant lamp. I prefer these hanging pendants in multiples, partially because the pendant kits only allow a 40-watt bulb.

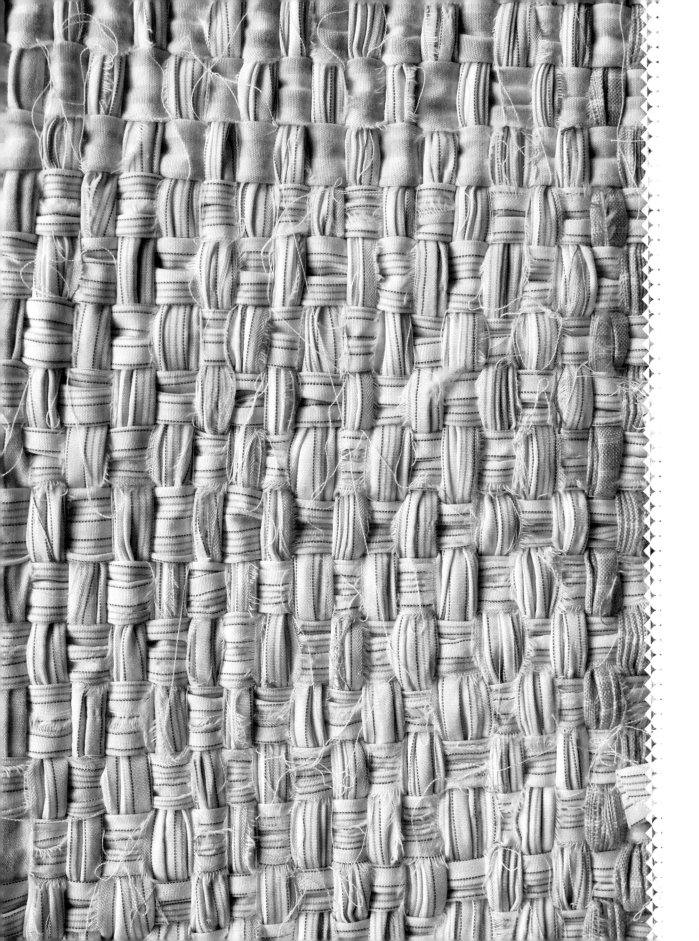

Woven Placemats

LEVEL
Beginner—no
sewing machine
required

MATERIALS
Men's dress
shirts and/or
bedsheets
in various colors/
patterns

**TOOLS AND
NOTIONS**
Scissors
Cork bulletin
board
Lots of pushpins

This is a project with an added therapeutic bonus, as it requires ripping up shirts and sheets, a wonderful outlet for any pent-up frustration you may have. Try it and you will see: This can do wonders for your state of mind. I came up with this craft when I remembered weaving strips of colored paper in kindergarten. This project is as simple as that, and it does not even require an actual loom: A simple cork bulletin board will do. Your finished placemat will be slightly smaller than the size of the board.

STEPS FOR WOVEN PLACEMATS

1. Measure the height and width of your cork board. Start ripping 1-in.-wide strips of fabric. The short ones will be your warp and should be about 10 in. longer than the height of your board; the long ones will be your weft and should be about 10 in. longer than the width of your board.

2. Fold the 1-in.-wide strips in half lengthwise to create doubled, ½-in.-wide strips. Place your board horizontally on a table. Pin the short strips vertically on the board about ½ in. apart, pinning right next to the top and bottom edge. Each strip will extend about 5 in. off the top and bottom of the board.

3. Start weaving the longer strips into this warp from the bottom up, again making sure that there is about a 5-in. length at both the left and right sides. Pin the weft in place with a pushpin right next to the left and right edge.

4. After weaving each additional strip, pull the weft down with your hands as tightly as possible before pinning it into place.

5. If you are working with strips of different colors or patterns, you can create stripes or checks in the weave, or just go for a random multicolor pattern.

6. When your bulletin board is completely covered with your weave, start removing the warp pushpins, two at a time. Knot together the two ends with a double knot, remove the next two pushpins, knot again, and so on.

7. When all the warp ends are knotted, do the same for the weft. You can trim the ends or just leave them long.

VARIATION

YOU CAN USE THIS SAME TECHNIQUE TO make a table runner. In that case, you'll want the weft pieces to be a lot longer—that's where the bedsheets come in handy. Leave them at a 5-in. length on the left and much longer (basically the length of the sheet) on the right. Once you're done with weaving your first board, tie off the warp on the top and bottom, and tie off the weft at the left side only. Move the whole piece to the left, add another set of warp pieces, and start weaving with the longer ends of your weft. Repeat this process until your runner is the desired length.

Denim Trivets

LEVEL
Beginner—no sewing machine required

MATERIALS
Denim scraps, or about one large pair of adult jeans per trivet

TOOLS AND NOTIONS
Ruler
Pencil or tailor's chalk
Scissors
Glue gun and glue sticks
Large hose clamps (I used a 7-in.-diameter and a 5½-in.-diameter hose clamp)
Flathead screwdriver

I originally made this project as a way to recycle wine bottle corks, and it occurred to me that tightly rolled strips of denim would do the trick just as well. These trivets provide the perfect insulation for hot pots and will never scratch or damage your table surface in any way.

STEPS FOR DENIM TRIVETS

1. Cut multiple strips of denim that are about 2 in. wide and 20 in. long (though they can be of varying lengths).

2. Roll up the strips as tightly as you possibly can, securing them with little dabs of hot glue as you go along. Make sure that the end of the strip is glued down especially well.

3. For my 7-in.-diameter hose clamp, I made about 53 rolls. For the 5½-in.-diameter hose clamp, I made about 35 rolls.

4. Use a flathead screwdriver to enlarge your hose clamp as large as you can without actually opening it up.

5. Place as many denim rolls as you can inside the hose clamp; you may need to play with the configuration of the rolls to achieve the tightest fit. If necessary, make a few extra smaller rolls to fill in the holes.

6. Tighten the hose clamp with the screwdriver, making sure that it is positioned in the middle of the rolls. Done!

NOTE These trivets can also be made with a heavy corduroy or felt. Do make sure to always use a natural material such as cotton, linen, or wool. Synthetic materials such as nylon and polyester will melt when coming in contact with extremely hot surfaces.

Bath Mat

LEVEL
Beginner—
sewing machine
required

MATERIALS
Karate belts: 2 brown,
2 orange, 2 yellow,
3 blue
Grippies® no-slip
patches or a
similar product

**TOOLS AND
NOTIONS**
Scissors
Sewing machine and
thread to match the
colors of the belts
Needle and thread

You come across the strangest things at flea markets. A few years ago, I bought a huge bag of karate belts in a rainbow of colors for $5. Was the martial arts school going out of business? I don't know, and I sure did not know what I was going to do with 40 karate belts. They sat in my closet forever, until I started working on this book. Then it hit me: The fun colors, the cushioned cotton, the absorbent material—this was going to be an awesome bath mat.

STEPS FOR BATH MAT

1. Cut the following 29-in. lengths: 4 brown and 4 orange karate belts. Cut the following 17-in. lengths: 4 yellow and 9 blue karate belts.

2. Using thread of a matching color, zigzag back and forth several times over all edges to prevent fraying.

3. Start the weaving process with the first blue piece: Place the brown and orange

pieces next to each other and "weave" the blue piece (over-under-over-under) through them, leaving about a 2-in. piece sticking out at either end.

4. Wherever the bands are crossing, hand-sew the pieces together with a few stitches.

5. Now, weave in the next blue piece and repeat the process.

6. When you are done with the blue pieces, do the same with the yellow pieces.

7. Finally, stick a handful of stick-on Grippies or a similar product to the back of the mat to prevent slipping.

NOTE Here's a fun variation on the above project, using nylon seat belt webbing, which can be bought at automotive centers and online in a wide variety of colors and widths. Follow all steps as described above, except for step 2 because the nylon will not fray.

Indigo Bench

LEVEL
Intermediate—sewing machine required

MATERIAL
Vintage bench or chair with rush seat
Denim remnants or one pair of jeans

TOOLS AND NOTIONS
Box cutter
Sandpaper
Wood stain
Brush
Seam ripper
Ruler
Pencil or tailor's chalk
Scissors
Sewing machine and thread
Upholstery tacks
Hammer

When I came across this dusty old bench in a Salvation Army store in Upstate New York, I knew it had my name on it. I paid $9.99. Inspired by its trapezoidal shape and graceful spindles, I envisioned a rustic Japanese look for my upgrade.

STEPS FOR BENCH

1. Vintage rush seats often become brittle with age, so the rushing is usually quite easy to remove. Use a box cutter if necessary. You may want to do this outside, as it will be a messy and dusty process.

2. Once all the rushing has been removed, thoroughly sand the bench, first with a rough sandpaper, then with a finer grit.

3. Brush off all the dust, and clean with a damp cloth. If any structural repairs need to be made to the bench, now is the time to do this.

4. Once the bench is completely dry, brush on a coat of wood stain in the color of your choice. I used Minwax® in Ebony.

5. Open up the inside leg seam of the jeans with a seam ripper, press it flat, and cut out long, vertical 1-in.-wide strips.

6. Join the strips together by overlapping them by about ½ in. at the ends and stitching several times back and forth over both layers.

7. Once you have a long length of denim strips, you can start weaving. First attach the end in the corner on the underside of the bench by nailing it in place with two upholstery tacks. Do not use regular thumbtacks, as they will not be strong enough.

8. Wrap the strips tightly all around the bench, until the entire seat is covered. This will be your warp. Cut off your strip and secure underneath the bench with two more upholstery tacks.

9. Now repeat the process for the weft, only weave the strips—over-under-over-under —through the warp. Make sure both ends are secured tightly with upholstery tacks.

   NOTE This bench has quickly become the favorite perch of my newly adopted kitten, Ollie—the best kind of endorsement!

4 GIFTS

AS MUCH AS I LOVE Christmas and other gift-giving occasions, there is something about the surrounding spending frenzy that really turns me off. Gift buying can rapidly turn into a meaningless and obligatory chore, devoid of thought and care. I have been guilty of this many times myself. One way to combat this is to produce a handmade gift. Even if it is not perfect, its recipient will treasure and appreciate it so much more for the time, effort, and thought you put into it.

Cup Holders

LEVEL

Intermediate—sewing machine required

MATERIALS

Thick fabric scraps (I used a sample of an all-over crewel embroidery. Velvets and heavy corduroys would work great, too.)

1-in.-wide double-fold bias tape

TOOLS AND NOTIONS

Cardboard cup (for making template)

Pencil or tailor's chalk

Scissors

Sewing machine and thread

Iron

This may sound a bit strange, but from the point of view of someone who did not grow up in New York (or anywhere else in this wonderful country), there are a few things that used to strike me as very exotic, very cool, very NYC: yellow taxicabs, steam rising from the streets, the smell of roasted peanuts. Another is the whole coffee-to-go street culture. Growing up in Belgium, you did not see people walking on the street in the morning with coffee in paper cups. There is unfortunately a wasteful aspect to this chic cosmopolitan practice. Even if you can't always bring your own cup, you can make your own reusable and completely customized cup holder instead of using a disposable one.

STEPS FOR CUP HOLDERS

1. You can easily make your own template by simply cutting open a paper coffee cup, flattening out the sides, and tracing the shape onto template paper or your desired fabric. Do this and cut out the fabric, adding a ½-in. seam allowance to each end.

95

2. Sew the side seams together by placing good side to good side. Press the seams down and turn the cup holder good side out.

3. Fold out one side of your bias tape and pin, aligning the edge with the top edge of your cup holder. Machine-stitch right in the crease of the tape. This is somewhat tricky, as you likely won't be able to fit the cup holder around the "arm" of your sewing machine. Take your time to do this; it may even help to loosely stitch the tape into place by hand, before going over it with the machine.

4. Now fold the bias tape over the top edge of your cup holder, and stitch in place by hand on the inside. Remove the pins. See p. 15 for a step-by-step tutorial on how to sew on bias tape. Repeat steps 3 and 4 for the bottom edge of your cup holder.

NOTE This is a wonderful project to make in duplicates for selling at craft fairs or school fundraisers, especially when there is a focus on sustainability.

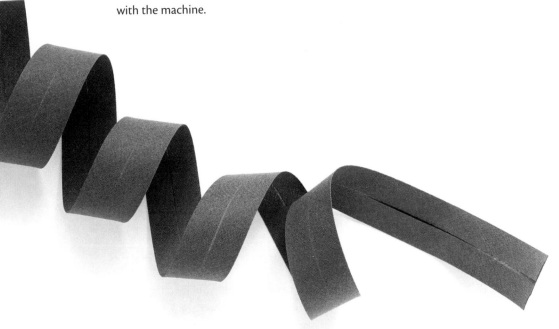

Tie Wrap

LEVEL
Intermediate—sewing machine required

MATERIALS
12 striped silk men's ties
1 yd. striped silk fabric (for the lining of the wrap)
Twin-size (72-in. by 90-in.) lightweight quilt batting

TOOLS AND NOTIONS
Seam ripper
Iron
Scissors
Ruler
Pencil or tailor's chalk
Pins
Sewing machine and thread

During a period of self-inflicted unemployment a number of years ago, I really felt the need to make something with my hands. My funds for materials were limited, however, which is how I found myself at a Salvation Army in the city buying up its entire stock of men's silk ties at 50 cents apiece. I had no idea what I was going to do with them, but I just knew the colors and material appealed to me. It was only when I saw tie silk by the yard in a fabric store that it all came together: I was going to make a padded silk wrap.

STEPS FOR TIE WRAP

1. Using a seam ripper, carefully undo the stitching on the back of each tie. Remove and discard the lining and interfacing and press the silk flat.

2. Cut the ties into 14-in.-long pieces and place them on the floor, right side up, to figure out a pleasing pattern and color combination. In order to end up with a rectangular wrap, you will need to alternate the direction of the pieces: wide to narrow, narrow to wide, and so on.

3. Once you have figured out the right layout, pin all the pieces together, good side to good side, and machine-stitch them together with a ½-in. seam allowance.

to good side. Machine-stitch together, remove pins, and press open seams.

7. Now place the wrap front on the floor, good side up, layer the lining on top of it, good side down, and finally place the batting on top of that. Pin all three layers together on the marked pencil line and stitch all around, except for one of the 12-in. sides.

8. Remove the pins. Open up the three layers of seam allowance and cut down the batting seam allowance as close as you can, without cutting into the stitching.

9. Carefully cut off the seam corners diagonally (as shown on p. 13), making sure not to cut into the stitching.

10. Press open the seams and turn the wrap inside out. Gently push out and shape each corner with the point of your scissors from the inside. Press flat with an iron, then pin and hand-stitch the last remaining 12-in. opening shut. Remove the pins.

11. Machine-stitch all around the edge of the wrap ⅛ in. away from the edge, using a thread in a coordinating color.

NOTE When you pick out the ties, it helps to follow a general color palette. I stuck to a "shades of red" color family. The patchwork of stripes can be quite a graphic statement, so sticking to one overall color will tie it all together—pun intended! If you cannot find a striped silk by the yard for the back, you can substitute with a color-coordinated silk satin or shantung, both of which are usually available in a wide range of shades.

4. Remove the pins. Press open all the seams on the back. Using a ruler and pencil, mark up a rectangle on the back of this patchworked piece that is 12 in. wide by 84 in. long. This completes the front of the wrap.

5. Using a pencil and ruler, mark up a rectangle on the batting that is 12 in. wide by 84 in. long. Cut out with a ½-in. seam allowance all around.

6. Using a pencil and ruler, mark up three rectangles that are 12 in. wide by 28 in. long on the back of the lining fabric. Cut out with a ½-in. seam allowance all around and pin the 12-in. sides together, good side

Lavender Cubes

LEVEL
Intermediate—sewing machine required

MATERIALS
Old pair of jeans
Dried lavender

TOOLS AND NOTIONS
Cardboard
Ruler
Iron
Pencil or tailor's chalk
Scissors
Sewing machine and thread
Paper and clear tape
Needle and thread

When you have rapidly growing kids, jeans are a wardrobe staple. After they've served their second term as cutoffs in the summer, I turn them into these scented lavender cubes, which look great when grouped together on a coffee table. They are very sturdy, so they can easily be tossed around in any wardrobe, sock drawer, coat closet, you name it, to keep things smelling fresh and to naturally repel moths. In order to revive the scent, just squeeze the cube every once in a while.

STEPS FOR LAVENDER CUBES

1. Make a cardboard template that's 5 in. by 5 in. Recycled cereal boxes provide the perfect template material.

2. Cut open the inside leg seams of your jeans and lay the fabric flat; press with a hot iron if needed.

3. Place the template on the wrong side of the denim and mark with a pencil, with the edges parallel to the weave—do not draw the squares on the bias. You can include details such as pockets and grommets in the squares if you like.

4. Cut out six squares for each cube on the pencil lines; no need for a seam allowance.

5. Attach the squares to each other—both good sides of the fabric should be facing

out—with a zigzag machine stitch, going back and forth several times. Make sure to use a heavy-duty denim needle on your machine. The first five squares should be sewn together in a cross pattern. Then stitch the sides together to form a cube. Finally, attach the "lid" of the cube.

6. When stitching the last seam, leave half of it undone. Make a funnel out of a piece of paper and some tape and use it to fill the cube with dried lavender. Try to pack in as much lavender as you can. The rest of the seam will need to be stitched closed by hand, as it is hard to use the machine once the cube is filled.

NOTE As an alternative to lavender, you can also fill the cubes with dried chamomile flowers (relaxing and stress relieving), dried rosemary (repels mice and insects), or dried pine needles (refreshing). If you choose pine needles, do make sure your fabric is sturdy and thick enough—a denim should work fine—as you don't want the needles to poke through.

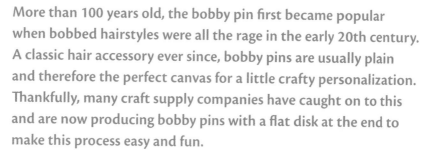

Yo-Yo Hairpins

LEVEL
Beginner—no sewing machine required

MATERIALS
Lightweight silk or cotton scraps
Small buttons

TOOLS AND NOTIONS
Cups and bowls to use as templates
Pencil or tailor's chalk
Scissors
Needle and thread
Bobby pins with a disk
Strong glue

More than 100 years old, the bobby pin first became popular when bobbed hairstyles were all the rage in the early 20th century. A classic hair accessory ever since, bobby pins are usually plain and therefore the perfect canvas for a little crafty personalization. Thankfully, many craft supply companies have caught on to this and are now producing bobby pins with a flat disk at the end to make this process easy and fun.

STEPS FOR YO-YO HAIRPINS

1. Thinner fabrics such as tie silks and shirting cottons work best for making yo-yos. I used vintage silk ties, which I opened up with a seam ripper and pressed flat before using.

2. Using various lids, bowls, and cups as templates, mark circles on the back of the silk

103

fabric with a pencil. Bear in mind that the template's diameter needs to be twice the diameter of the finished yo-yo. For the hairpins, I made yo-yos in two sizes: My templates were 4½ in. and 3½ in. in diameter.

3. Thread your needle and make a double knot at the end. Hand-sew a small up-and-down stitch all around the perimeter of your fabric circle, about ¼ in. from the edge.

4. Gently cinch the whole thing together, pushing over the unfinished edges toward the inside of the yo-yo. Now, flatten the yo-yo so that the cinched part is in the center, and secure in place with a few stitches.

5. Layer the small yo-yo on top of the large one and place a small button on top. Hand-sew them all together, going through the button and through both yo-yos.

6. Finally, attach the yo-yo to the disk of the bobby pin with a small dab of strong glue. Make sure the glue dries for at least three hours before using. These make a great gift set, slipped onto a greeting card.

NOTE Of course, there are many more fun uses for yo-yos. As shown in the photo at left, I have strategically sewn on a few color-coordinated silk ones to hide the moth holes on a vintage cashmere cardigan. Traditionally, these yo-yos were sewn together to make bedspreads—popular in the 1930s and 1940s—or even jackets. If you don't quite have the patience for that, a smaller quantity can make for a really pretty scarf. Since yo-yos are made from relatively small pieces of fabric, this is also a highly portable project, thus the perfect travel craft.

Cool Tops

LACE TOP

Here are three easy ways to customize a simple sleeveless undershirt into a truly one-of-kind item, the perfect gift for a special little girl in your life. I used a boys' size small for an 8-year-old girl, so feel free to dabble between the departments of your local shops to find something that suits you!

LEVEL
Intermediate—no sewing machine required

MATERIALS
One white sleeveless undershirt

Vintage crochet doilies and edgings

TOOLS AND NOTIONS
Iron

Pins

Needle

Thread

Scissors

STEPS FOR LACE TOP

1. Iron the undershirt and place it flat on your work surface.

2. Position doilies and edgings on the front of the shirt until you have found a pleasing arrangement. This can be quite the puzzle! You can overlap pieces slightly if needed.

3. Once you are happy with the layout, pin the pieces in place, making sure you only pin them to the front of the shirt, not the back.

4. Using needle and thread, hand-sew all items in place, using tiny little hemstitches (as described on p. 12) all around each crochet piece. This is a time-consuming process, but the smaller your stitches are, the more secure and long-lasting the final result will be.

FRINGE TOP

LEVEL	TOOLS AND NOTIONS
Beginner—no sewing machine required	Iron
	Scissors
MATERIALS	Pins
One white sleeveless undershirt	Needle
Plain white T-shirt or a quarter yard of white jersey fabric	Thread

STEPS FOR FRINGE TOP

1. Iron the undershirt and place it flat on the work surface.

2. Cut the body of the T-shirt into vertical strips that are 5 in. wide.

3. Cut each strip horizontally into ¼-in.-wide fringe, leaving only ½ in. at one side uncut.

4. Fold the fringe lengthwise backward by 1 in., and then forward by 1 in., in an accordion-like fashion and pin in place. Repeat this process for the entire length. The fringe will now be three layers thick. Starting at the shirt's shoulder seam, hand-sew the now tripled fringe onto the outer edge of the neckline binding.

5. When you run out of fringe, just start a new piece, no need to attach both pieces of fringe to each other.

6. Repeat the process to attach a triple layer of fringe to the inner edge of the neckline binding.

7. Last step: Tie a single knot into every single fringe strip, about 1 in. from the end.

FLOWER TOP

LEVEL

Beginner—no sewing machine required

MATERIALS

One white sleeveless undershirt

Light- to medium-weight cotton scraps, in various coordinated colors

TOOLS AND NOTIONS

Round plates and bowls to use as templates

Pencil or tailor's chalk

Scissors

Needle and thread

4 button-making kits (my buttons were 1½ in. in diameter)

STEPS FOR FLOWER TOP

1. Using various sizes of bowls and plates as templates, mark three sizes of circles on the back of the fabric scraps with a pencil. Bear in mind that the template's diameter needs to be roughly twice the diameter of the finished yo-yo. My templates were 5 in., 6½ in., and 8¼ in. in diameter. Cut out four fabric circles of each size.

2. Thread your needle and make a double knot at the end. Hand-sew a small up-and-down stitch all around the perimeter of your fabric circle, about ¼ in. from the edge.

3. Gently cinch the whole thing together, pushing over the unfinished edges toward the inside of the yo-yo. Now, flatten the yo-yo so that the cinched part is in the center, and secure with a few stitches.

4. Follow the instructions of your button-making kit: Cut out a fabric circle following the kit's template, pop it in the mold with the good side down, put in the button top with the good side down, fold over the fabric edges, and clip on the button bottom.

5. Layer one yo-yo of each size on top of each other (largest on the bottom) and place the fabric-covered button on top. Hand-sew them all together, going through the button's shank and through all three yo-yos. Don't cut off the thread yet.

6. With the same thread, secure the corsage with a few stitches to the shirt: three on the left shoulder and one on the right.

Princess Crown

LEVEL
Beginner—no sewing machine required

MATERIALS
Remnant of heavy guipure lace or crochet edging

TOOLS AND NOTIONS
Cardboard mailing tube, 3¼ in. in diameter
Duct tape
Ruler
Scissors
Needle and thread
Mod Podge
Paintbrush
Gold paint (I used the kind meant for painting model cars)
Bobby pins

This will sound pompous, but I will say it anyway: The greatest gift you can give a child is the gift of play and imagination. These princess crowns are a wonderful addition to the dressing-up box. It's so important to nurture creativity early in life, and pretend play does just that. These precious crowns will make any child feel like royalty. And they aren't just for girls; don't be afraid to upsize them for your little prince.

STEPS FOR PRINCESS CROWNS

1. Cover the cardboard mailing tube with a few strips of duct tape, to prevent the crown from permanently getting stuck to it.

2. Cut your lace edging to a length of about 11 in.

3. Using needle and thread, hand-sew the ends together around the tube. Don't worry too much about fraying ends; the Mod Podge will take care of that.

4. Brush on a thick coat of Mod Podge; by dabbing your brush onto the lace, you will make all the details in the lace come out.

5. Once your first coat is dry, dab on a second coat.

6. Once the second coat has fully dried (this can take up to 24 hours), gently remove the lace crown from the mailing tube. Use the sharp end of a knife if necessary.

7. Use a needle to punch through any lace bits that may have accidentally been painted "shut" by the Mod Podge, and make sure to poke a few holes on the bottom edge of the crown large enough for a bobby pin to fit through.

8. Paint the inside and outside of the crown gold and let dry.

9. Secure in hair with a few bobby pins.

NOTE A similar technique can be used to make a treasure chest filled with "gold" bangles. Just make sure to use a mold that has the right diameter: too small and the bangles won't fit over your wrist, too big and they will slip right off your arm.

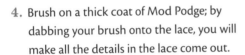

Coin Purse

LEVEL
Intermediate—sewing machine required

MATERIALS
Medium-weight cotton or linen scraps for the outside of the purse (avoid heavier weights, as they will prevent proper closure of the purse)

Lightweight silk or cotton scraps (for the lining)

Metal snap purse frame (I used a sew-on purse frame with prepunched holes, see pp. 133–135 for resources)

TOOLS AND NOTIONS
Cardboard
Pencil or tailor's chalk
Scissors
Pins
Sewing machine and thread
Iron
Heavy-duty thread
Needle

Though it may seem crass, for certain occasions, the gift of cash is really the most appreciated. If you are truly unsure of what to give someone, money can be the best alternative. In fact, giving small amounts of money to kids can be a valuable educational tool. But that doesn't mean your gift has to lack a personal touch. A pretty coin purse in the recipient's favorite color or pattern is the perfect gift wrap.

STEPS FOR COIN PURSE

1. My purse frame kit came with a template of the frame. If yours does not, place the frame on cardboard and trace the outside. Make sure to mark the bottom of the frame hinges.

2. Draw the shape of the rest of the purse in the shape and size you desire.

3. Using this template, cut out two pieces of outer fabric and two pieces of lining. Make sure to mark the bottom of the frame hinges on the fabric. Cut them all out with a ½-in. seam allowance all around.

4. Place outer fabric pieces on top of each other, good side to good side, and pin. Machine-stitch the frame body, going from frame hinge to frame hinge. Repeat this process for the lining pieces.

5. If your purse body has curved edges—like mine—make V-shaped cuts in the seam allowance (as described on p. 14).

6. Turn the outer piece good side out and insert into the lining (which is still wrong side out).

7. Pin the purse frame edges to each other on both sides and machine-stitch together, leaving a 2½-in. opening. Again, make small V-shaped cuts in the seam allowance.

8. Pull the outer piece through the 2½-in. opening, and push the lining into place. Pin and hand-sew the opening shut, and press. Remove the pins

9. Finally, insert the finished edges on both sides into the purse frame and hand-sew in place. I used a heavier-duty thread for this, knowing that this attachment needs to be really secure.

NOTE If there are no holes in the frame to sew through, you will need to apply a heavy-duty glue inside the frame before inserting the purse's edges. A flathead screwdriver will come in handy at this point to push the fabric into place. Make sure you let the glue dry for at least a full day before using the purse.

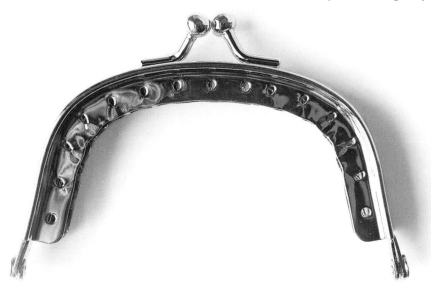

Tassels

LEVEL
Beginner—no
sewing machine
required

MATERIALS
Old horizontally
striped T-shirts

**TOOLS AND
NOTIONS**
Ruler
Scissors
Key chain hardware

I made these tassels out of some much-beloved striped T-shirts, now too small for my kids to wear. They are among the easiest and quickest crafts to make in this book and have so many fun uses: key chains; adornments for backpacks, suitcases, and purses; curtain tie-backs; even necklaces!

STEPS FOR TASSELS

1. Cut both the front and back of your T-shirts into ¼-in.-wide strips that are about 12 in. to 15 in. long, following the "grain" of the jersey fabric—so cut from top to bottom, not from left to right.

2. Gather your strips and fold over through the loop of the hardware. Fit through as many strips as you can for a nice, full tassel.

3. Tie the strips together underneath with an extra fabric strip, and make sure to double-knot.

4. Give your tassel a "haircut" to make sure all the strips are a similar length.

   NOTE The tassel on the facing page (bottom middle) was made with tiny strips of silk. The fraying is part of the "undone" look—embrace it!

Drawstring Bags

LEVEL
Beginner—sewing machine required

MATERIALS
Linen remnant for outside of bag
Lightweight velvet or silk remnant for lining of bag
Linen or satin ribbon, ¾ in. wide and 30 in. long

TOOLS AND NOTIONS
Ruler
Pencil or tailor's chalk
Scissors
Pins
Sewing machine and thread
Safety pin

Here's another example of the gift wrap being part of the gift. You can make drawstring bags in any size, shape, or color, and they can hold a wide variety of items: wine bottles, gourmet food, a pretty pair of slippers, a set of beauty products. I personally love the visual surprise of a bag that is neutral on the outside, yet lined with a bold and bright color on the inside. Shy away from using heavy- or upholstery-weight velvet, as it will be much too thick to gather together with the drawstring.

STEPS FOR DRAWSTRING BAGS

1. With ruler and pencil, mark up a rectangle on the back side of the outer fabric that is 22 in. wide by 13½ in. long. Cut it out with a ½-in. seam allowance all around.

2. Repeat this process for the lining fabric.

3. Fold the outer fabric over vertically, good side to good side. Pin and sew the bottom and side seams. Cut off the corner of the seam allowance diagonally (as described on p. 13) and press open seams.

4. Repeat this process for the lining fabric.

5. Turn the outer piece good side out and insert into the lining (which is still wrong side out). Pin the top edges together, and sew together, leaving a 4-in. opening on one side.

6. Pull the outer piece through the 4-in. opening, and push the lining into place. Pin, hand-sew the opening shut, and press.

7. Machine-stitch a straight line, all across the top of the bag, 1 in. from the edge.

8. Cut a 30-in.-long piece of ribbon, attach a safety pin to one end, and use that to feed it through the opening. Make sure to hold on to the other end of the ribbon. Once the ribbon has been fed all the way through, make a single knot on either end and hand-sew the 4-in. opening shut, leaving only a 1-in. opening for both ribbon ends to come out.

NOTE After the gift itself has been put to good use, the bags can serve other purposes, too. I made some of the bags here with a lightweight velvet lining, knowing they would make the perfect luxury shoe bags for traveling. The above size is perfect for a size 8 women's shoe. This truly is the gift that keeps on giving.

Cats

LEVEL
Beginner—no
sewing machine
required

MATERIALS
Stray baby/kid socks
Small buttons

**TOOLS AND
NOTIONS**
Scissors
Needle
Thread
Uncooked rice
Pins
Glue gun and
glue sticks
Jute twine or
embroidery floss

It is remarkable how many stray socks you end up with in a family of four. I mean, really, do they breed in the dryer? Here's a fun way to recycle them. These cats were inspired by one of my favorite magical cartoon cat characters. I came up with this project so kids of all ages can create their very own cat characters, magic and all.

STEPS FOR CATS

1. Cut off the foot of your sock so you end up with a piece of knit tube.

2. Thread your needle and make a double knot at the end. Hand-sew a small up-and-down stitch all around the unfinished edge of the sock.

3. Cinch the whole thing together, turn the unfinished edge toward the inside, and secure with a few more stitches.

4. Turn the sock upside down and fill it up with uncooked rice. The more rice you use, the fatter your cat will be.

5. Flatten the top of the sock, pin it in place, and close with a simple hemstitch. To mark the ears, hand-sew a little up-and-down stitch in a diagonal direction on either side.

6. Hot-glue two buttons on the face and stitch two pieces of knotted twine or embroidery floss underneath the eyes.

Mice

LEVEL
Beginner—sewing
machine required

Since I put a cat project in this book, it seemed logical to make some mice as well. These cat toys are the perfect gift for any cat owner (or should that be for any cat?), though I will warn you: If you make these in muted gray colors, as I did, they can be mistaken for the real thing!

MATERIAL
Remnant of light- to
medium-weight
chenille or velvet
Small felt scraps
Thin elastic ribbon, or
shoelace

**TOOLS AND
NOTIONS**
Cardboard for
templates
Pencil or tailor's chalk
Scissors
Pins
Sewing machine
and thread
Paper and tape
Uncooked rice
Needle and thread

and sew across the curved line of the back. Make a series of V-shaped cuts into the seam allowance, as shown on p. 14.

3. Pin the resulting piece, good side on good side, to the mouse bottom. Pin together and sew all around, except for a 2½-in. space at the back end. Remove the pins. Make a series of V-shaped cuts into the seam allowance and cut down the seam allowance to about ⅜ in.

STEPS FOR MICE

1. Using the templates on p. 130, mark up one mouse bottom and two mouse bodies (flip the pattern piece for the second body piece) on the wrong side of the chenille fabric. Cut them out with a ½-in. seam allowance all around.

2. Place the two body pieces on top of each other, good side to good side, pin together,

4. Turn the mouse inside out. Make a funnel with a piece of paper and tape, and use it to fill the mouse with uncooked rice (and maybe just a bit of catnip).

5. Hand-sew the 2½-in. opening shut, and make sure to include a 10-in. length of elastic ribbon (or half a shoelace) in the stitching. This will be the tail.

6. Using the ear template, mark up and cut out two felt ears; no need for a seam allowance on these.

7. Fold the bottom of each ear over, and stitch together with a few hand stitches. Do not cut off the thread just yet.

8. Using the same needle and thread, hand-sew both ears to the front of the mouse body.

NOTE As an alternative to rice, the mouse can be filled with batting, which will make it lighter and easier for cats to bat around.

Beaded Bugs

LEVEL
Intermediate—sewing machine required

MATERIALS
Denim scraps (for the top of the beetle)
Silk or satin scraps (for the beetle's belly)
Sequins
Seed and bugle beads

TOOLS AND NOTIONS
Cardboard for templates
Pencil or tailor's chalk
Scissors
Pins
Sewing machine and thread
Uncooked rice
Needle and thread

This project took shape while we were sitting out a summer hurricane on Block Island, Rhode Island, and extreme boredom set in. I had brought along some embroidery supplies and, totally unrelated, a book on entomology. Also, my husband had just decided to turn his old jeans into shorts. I used the denim remnants to make Fred, the blue-green beetle. While I started looking at the entomology book for inspiration, I veered wildly off course and came up with some creatures entirely my own—so much more fun than following the rules.

STEPS FOR BUGS

1. For the blue-green beetle, cut out two body pieces, one in denim and one in silk, following the template on p. 131. Cut out with a ½-in. seam allowance all around.

2. Place the two pieces on top of each other, good side to good side. Pin and sew together on the pattern line, leaving a 1½-in. opening. Make a series of V-shaped cuts in the seam allowance, as described on p. 14.

3. Turn the beetle body inside out, fill it with rice (not too full), and sew shut by hand. The silk or satin side is the belly of the beetle.

4. Tie off the head by wrapping a piece of string several times around the body about 1 in. from the top.

5. Sew a variety of overlapping green and blue sequins on the top half of the body and head only.

6. Make a double knot in a sturdy (or double) thread, and string on the following: 1 seed bead, 2 bugle beads, 1 seed bead, and 2 bugle beads, and sew this onto the body's side for a leg. I gave Fred six legs.

7. The antennae are composed of 1 seed bead, 1 bugle bead, 1 seed bead, and 3 bugle beads.

NOTE The black creature on the bottom of this page was created in a similar way, but he received an extra layer of black sequined wings in a simple wedge-like shape, which were covered in sequins and then hand-sewn in place, right underneath the head. Above, the dragonfly's body has more of a carrot shape (again, filled with rice) and received two layers of wings, one slightly tucked underneath the other. Both layers are sewn underneath the head, perpendicular to the body. Templates for all three bugs can be found on pp. 131–132.

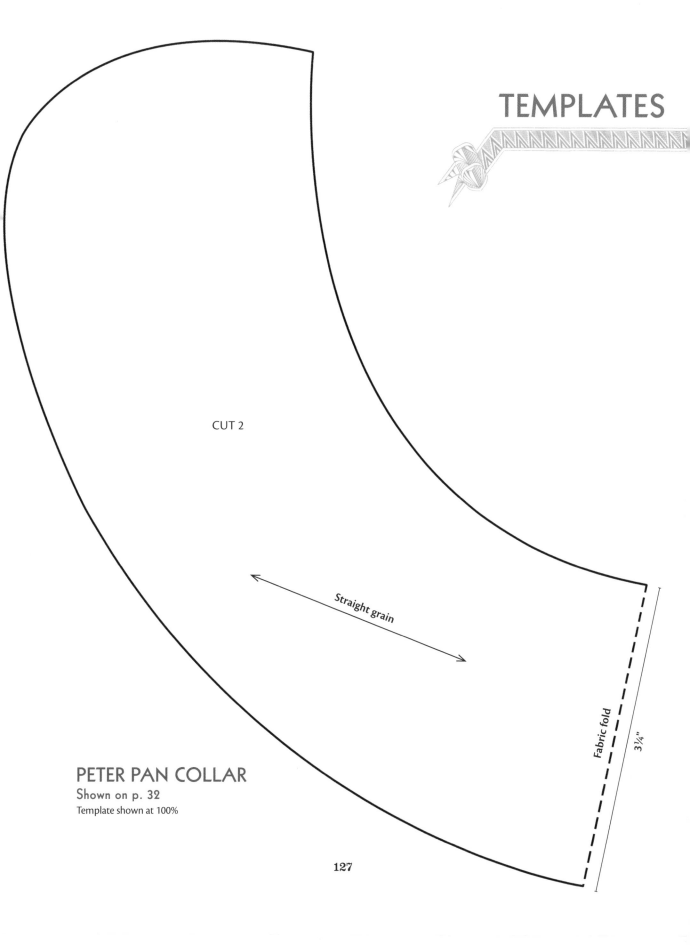

TEMPLATES

CUT 2

Straight grain

Fabric fold

3¼"

PETER PAN COLLAR
Shown on p. 32
Template shown at 100%

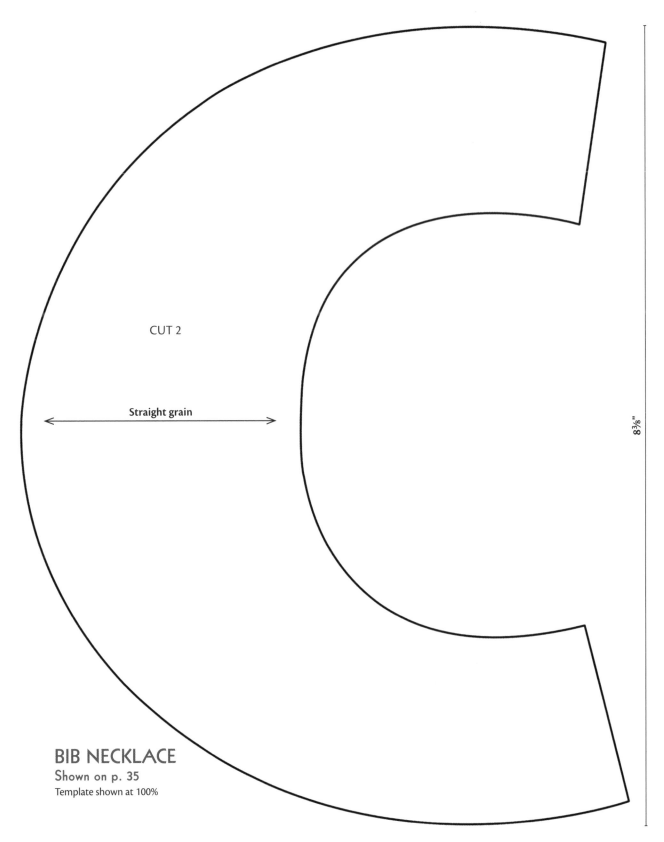

CUT 2

Straight grain

8⅜"

BIB NECKLACE
Shown on p. 35
Template shown at 100%

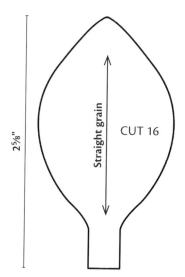

CORSAGE
Shown on p. 45
Template shown at 100%

$2^5/_8$"

Straight grain

CUT 16

1

$^3/_4$"

1"

T-JEWELRY
Shown on p. 48, p. 50, and p. 51

2   DETAIL

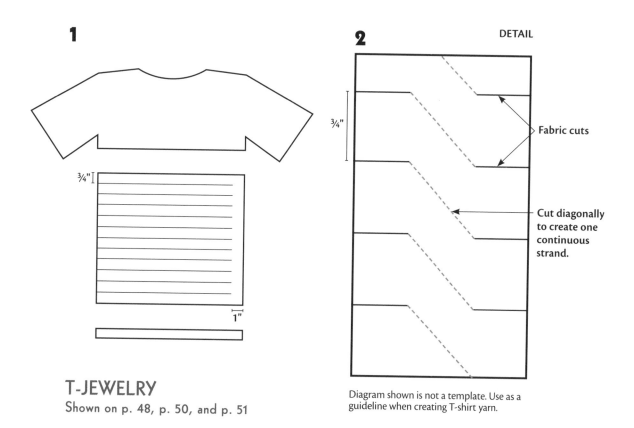

$^3/_4$"

Fabric cuts

Cut diagonally
to create one
continuous
strand.

Diagram shown is not a template. Use as a
guideline when creating T-shirt yarn.

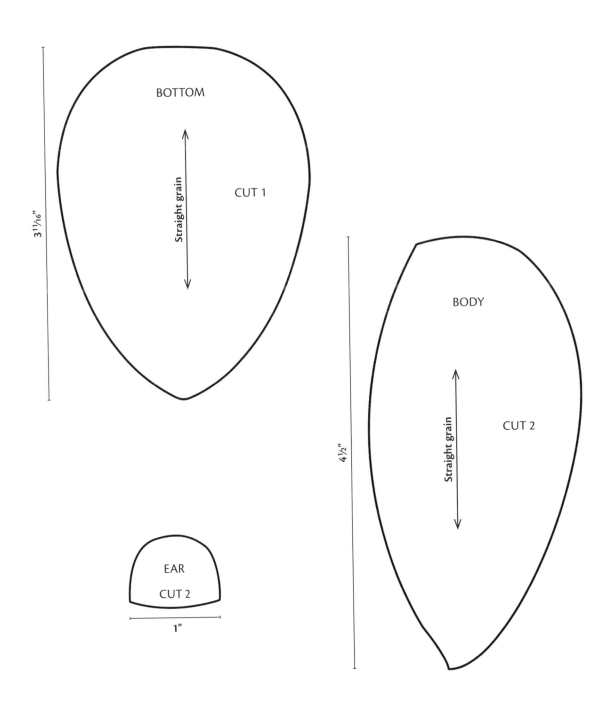

BOTTOM

CUT 1

Straight grain

$3^{11}/_{16}$"

BODY

CUT 2

Straight grain

$4^{1}/_{2}$"

EAR

CUT 2

1"

MICE
Shown on p. 123
Template shown at 100%

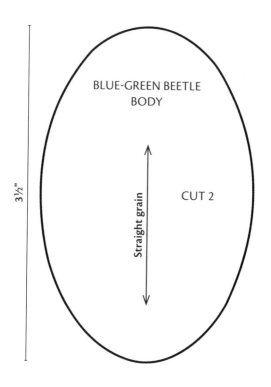

BLUE-GREEN BEETLE
BODY

Straight grain

CUT 2

3½"

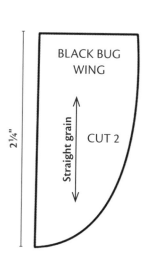

BLACK BUG
WING

Straight grain

CUT 2

2¼"

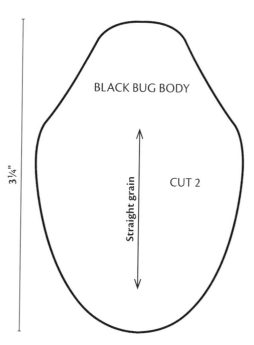

BLACK BUG BODY

Straight grain

CUT 2

3¼"

BEADED BUGS
Shown on p. 124 and p. 126
Template shown at 100%

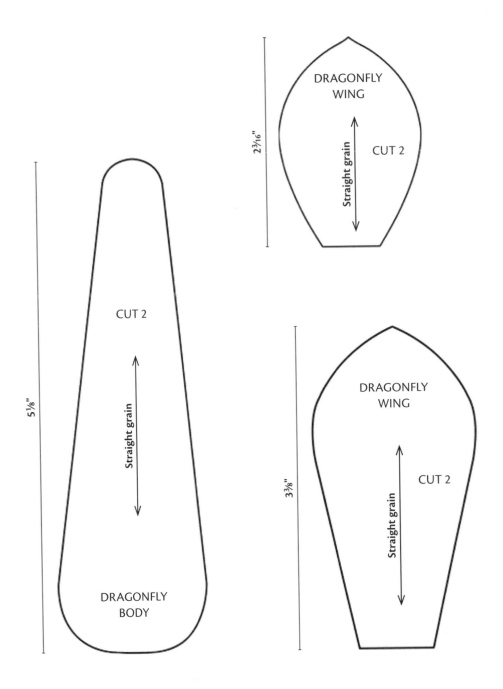

DRAGONFLY
WING

Straight grain

CUT 2

2³⁄₁₆"

CUT 2

Straight grain

DRAGONFLY
BODY

5⅛"

DRAGONFLY
WING

CUT 2

Straight grain

3³⁄₈"

BEADED BUGS

Shown on p. 126
Template shown at 100%

Materials and Tools

Calico More than 80 store locations, plus a comprehensive, recently revamped e-commerce site featuring more than 7,000 designer home textiles, trimmings, and more. http://www.calicocorners.com

Michaels North America's largest specialty retailer of arts and crafts for the hobbyist and do-it-yourself home decorator. http://www.michaels.com

A.C. Moore Arts and crafts superstores in the eastern United States, from Maine to Florida. http://www.acmoore.com

Hancock Fabrics Fabrics and craft and jewelry supplies. http://www.hancockfabrics.com

Beverly's Craft and fabric store selling online and in retail shops throughout California. http://www.beverlys.com

Jo-Ann Fabric and craft stores. http://www.joann.com

OnlineFabricStore Generally speaking, I prefer to do my fabric shopping in person— nothing beats going by touch and feel—but the selection on this website is so vast, it can't be beat. http://www.onlinefabricstore.net

Save on Crafts and **Create for Less** Two wonderful online outlets for great deals on a wide variety of craft supplies. http://www.save-on-crafts.com http://www.createforless.com

Lee's Art Shop and **Pearl Paint** Two of my favorite art supply stores. While nothing beats the actual physical environments (the smell of turpentine takes me right back to my art-school days), their websites are great as well. http://www.leesartshop.com http://www.pearlpaint.com

Freecycle and **Craigslist** Both websites facilitate selling, donating, or recycling a wide variety of items, through local classifieds and forums. https://www.freecycle.org http://www.craigslist.org

eBay and **Etsy** Both sites are great resources when you are hunting for really specific items or materials, both vintage and new. http://www.ebay.com https://www.etsy.com

Clover Clover is the manufacturer of a wide variety of knitting, crochet, needle art, sewing, quilting, and craft notions, including the Clover pom-pom maker. http://www.clover-usa.com

Tall Poppy Craft Products An e-commerce site, specifically offering a large selection of purse- and handbag-making supplies. http://www.tallpoppycraft.com

Brooklyn General Store and **Purl Soho**
Last but not least, when looking for craft materials and supplies, please do not overlook your local stores. Nothing beats the personal attention and customer service you'll receive. Plus, you'll join a local community of like-minded craftspeople and artists. Here are two of my personal favorites:

Brooklyn General Store's home within the old Frank's department store is a throwback/homage to another era. The vintage interior is not reproduced, just uncovered, cleaned, and painted. The store was created in an effort to provide the best-quality materials to a thriving crafters' community, and to promote making things by hand through inspiration and education. Check out their listing of classes online. I find myself making up any excuse to soak up the atmosphere in this magical place. http://brooklyngeneral.com

Purl Soho was created in 2002 as a friendly yarn shop, where people could gather and share each other's creativity. A few years later, Purl Patchwork, the fabric shop, joined the family, and since 2010, both stores live in one big, exciting space. The product selection is simply gorgeous. I want to live in this store. http://www.purlsoho.com

Flea Markets and Shows

Brimfield Antique and Collectibles Show
I may as well start with the mother of all flea markets: Brimfield, Massachusetts. More than 5,000 dealers congregate on several fields three times a year—what more can I say? My biggest tip is to book your accommodations well in advance. http://www.brimfieldshow.com

Elephant's Trunk Country Flea Market
The Elephant's Trunk Flea Market in New Milford, Connecticut, takes place every Sunday—weather permitting—roughly from Easter to Halloween. Check the website for weekly updates and get there early! On a Sunday morning, this is only an hour-and-a-half drive from New York City. http://www.etflea.com

Vintage Fashion and Textile Show This indoor show takes place in Sturbridge, Massachusetts, either during or the week before Brimfield. Touted as "the largest show of its type in the world," it's textile heaven. http://www.vintagefashionandtextileshow.com

Alameda Point Antiques Faire Held on the first Sunday of every month, this is the largest antiques show in northern California. Eight hundred dealer booths sell items that are 20 years old or older. http://www.alamedapointantiquesfaire.com

Giant Fall Flea Market in Ocean Grove, New Jersey This flea market traditionally takes place the weekend after Labor Day, in the picturesque town of Ocean Grove on the Jersey Shore. What better way to end the summer?
http://www.oceangrovenj.com/events.html

Marché aux Puces de Bruxelles Of course, I have to include the best flea market in Belgium. It takes place on the Vossenplein in the Marollen, an ancient working-class district in Belgium's capital, Brussels.
http://www.marcheauxpuces.be

Puces de Vanves The flea market in Clignancourt is the biggest, most famous of the Paris fleas. It is huge and overwhelming, and quite a few of the vendors cater to tourists. I prefer the quaint and much smaller flea near the Porte de Vanves subway stop. It's Paris at its best, and that includes the mouthwatering crêpe stands.
http://pucesdevanves.typepad.com

Braderie de Lilles Touted as the largest flea market of Europe, the Braderie de Lilles in the north of France is really more of a street festival, with lots of booths selling T-shirts, socks, gadgets, and—most of all—food! In fact, the signature dish of the day is mussels, and the restaurant that has the largest pile of empty mussel shells at the end of the weekend wins a prize. The booths selling vintage flea-market stuff are mostly on the outskirts of the town and away from the commercial center. Put on your walking shoes!
http://www.braderie-de-lille.fr

For Inspiration

ABC Home Unparalleled in the retail world, ABC Home offers six floors of choice at the cutting edge of design, beauty, and sustainability. Truly breathtaking and wildly inspiring, there is no place like (ABC) Home.
https://www.abchome.com

Melet Mercantile Aptly described as a "repository of dreams," Melet Mercantile's SoHo showroom—open by appointment only—is filled to the brink with choice vintage clothing, rare furniture, and cultural oddities.
http://www.meletmercantile.com

Hand/Eye The world's only journal dedicated to global creativity, focusing on the work of artists, artisans, designers, and other creatives, unfettered by traditional definitions of art, craft, and design. The articles and visuals will blow you away. Founder/editor Keith Recker also serves as the president of the HAND/EYE Fund, which operates a small grants fund for artisans worldwide.
http://handeyemagazine.com

METRIC EQUIVALENTS

One inch equals approximately
2.54 centimeters. To convert inches
to centimeters, multiply the figure in
inches by 2.54 and round off to the
nearest half centimeter, or use the chart
below, whose figures are rounded off
(1 centimeter equals 10 millimeters).

⅛ in. = 3 mm	9 in. = 23 cm
¼ in. = 6 mm	10 in. = 25.5 cm
⅜ in. = 1 cm	12 in. = 30.5 cm
½ in. = 1.3 cm	14 in. = 35.5 cm
⅝ in. = 1.5 cm	15 in. = 38 cm
¾ in. = 2 cm	16 in. = 40.5 cm
⅞ in. = 2.2 cm	18 in. = 45.5 cm
1 in. = 2.5 cm	20 in. = 51 cm
2 in. = 5 cm	21 in. = 53.5 cm
3 in. = 7.5 cm	22 in. = 56 cm
4 in. = 10 cm	24 in. = 61 cm
5 in. = 12.5 cm	25 in. = 63.5 cm
6 in. = 15 cm	36 in. = 92 cm
7 in. = 18 cm	45 in. = 114.5 cm
8 in. = 20.5 cm	60 in. = 152 cm

INDEX

Note: **Bold** page numbers refer to project templates.

About the Author

Born and raised in Belgium, Vera Vandenbosch is a graduate of the renowned fashion department at the Antwerp Royal Academy of Fine Arts. She worked as a stylist, writer, and photographer for a trend forecasting company in Paris. This was followed by a move to New York, where she spearheads the marketing initiatives of major home furnishings, textiles, and interior design companies. In her spare time, Vera shops at as many flea markets as possible, has at least a dozen craft projects going in various stages of completion, explores the wonderful world of digital photography, contemplates short films as a new hobby, and blogs at www.style-diaries.com. She is the author of two Taunton Press craft booklets: *Bungee Band Bracelets & More* and *Mini Macramé*.

Vera lives in Brooklyn with her husband, two children, two cats, two birds, and far too many craft supplies.